Goode's World Atlas, © Copyright 1987 by Rand McNally & Company,
R.L. 87-S-155

Enchantment of the World

ROMANIA

By Betty Carran

Consultant: Vladimir Tismaneanu, Ph.D., Foreign Policy Research Institute, Philadelphia, Pennsylvania

Consultant for Reading: Robert L. Hillerich, Ph.D., Bowling Green State University, Bowling Green, Ohio

CHILDRENS PRESS ®

CHICAGO

The traditional clothing worn by Romanians differs from region to region (above and opposite page).

Dedicated to Julie, my daughter-in-law. Her patience, encouragement and technical help were invaluable to me in completing this project.

In memory of Arthur Weitzner

Library of Congress Cataloging-in-Publication Data

Carran, Betty.
  Romania.

  (Enchantment of the world)
  Includes index.
  Summary: An introduction to the geography, history, government, economy, culture, and people of the only Eastern European country that traces its origins back to the Romans.
  1. Romania—Juvenile literature. [1. Romania]
I. Title. II. Series.
DR205.C28 1988   949.8   87-35423
ISBN 0-516-02703-4

FOURTH PRINTING, 1994.
Childrens Press®, Chicago
Copyright © 1988, 1993 by Childrens Press©, Inc.

Picture Acknowledgments
H. Armstrong Roberts: © E. Pozsonyi; 4, 12 (left), 56 (top), 74 (top left)
Shostal Associates: 10, 12 (right), 17, 40 (2 photos), 43, 44, 59, 68 (top), 71, 77 (right), 82 (left), 87 (left), 96 (top), 104; © Niklas Deak; 5, 8, 85 (bottom right), 95
Root Resources: © Jonathan & Mary Hagar; 6 (2 photos), 19, 20, 48 (bottom left), 55 (right), 60, 61 (2 photos), 67 (2 photos), 72, 77 (left), 81 (right), 82 (right), 85 (top and bottom left), 86 (left), 91, 96 (bottom), 100 (2 photos), 105; © Dr. Kramarz; 15, 16, 18, 21 (left), 22, 42, 51, 56 (bottom right), 63 (3 photos), 64, 81 (left), 86 (right); © Jane Shepstone; 52, 73 (right), 87 (right); © Constance S. Coning, 54
Valan Photos: © Aubrey Diem; 9 (left), 23, 47 (2 photos), 48 (top), 57 (left), 68 (bottom), 73 (left), 88 (right); © M.G. Kingshott; 74 (bottom right); © Helen C. Howes; 49 (right)
© **Betty Carran:** Cover, 9 (right), 21 (right), 49 (left), 50 (left), 53, 58, 65 (2 photos), 74 (top right and bottom left), 88 (left), 89, 117, 118
Historical Pictures Service, Chicago: 26 (2 photos), 31 (2 photos)
AP/Wide World Photos: 24, 33, 34 (2 photos), 37, 38, 101 (left), 102
Third Coast Stock Source: © Ted H. Funk; 48 (bottom right), 50 (right), 56 (bottom left), 57 (right), 76, 79, 83 (2 photos), 92, 93 (right), 94, 99, 101 (right)
Photri: 55 (left); © A. Novak; 93 (left)
Journalism Services Inc.: © John M. Nallon; 90
Len W. Meents: Maps on pages 10, 45, 62
Courtesy Flag Research Center, Winchester, Massachusetts 01890: Flag on back cover
Cover: A view of Peatre Neamt in Moldavia

TABLE OF CONTENTS

Left: Storks build their nests atop the chimneys. Below: The countryside in the region of Moldavia and Bukovina

Chapter 1

PEAKS, PLAINS, AND PLATEAUS

History recounts a bitter story of struggle and torture, hardship and foreign occupation that preceded the formation of Romania as we know it today. For centuries, it was the crossroads of barbarian invasions, the object of exploitation and brutal domination by a succession of aspiring empire builders.

The original Dacian settlers, a part of the Thracian tribe from the Eastern Balkans, were followed by Romans and Greeks, Goths, Huns and Tatars, Hungarians and Germans, Turks, Poles, Austrians, and Russians surging back and forth in migrations and conquests. Romania's borders have expanded and contracted in accordance with treaties and alliances throughout history.

In spite of this troubled past, Romania has emerged as a land of painted monasteries and fairy-tale castles. It is a land of emerald-green forests, the blue-brown Danube River, towering mountains, and gentle rolling plains. Thatch-roofed cottages with nesting storks and peasants in native costumes in the countryside are contrasted with high-rise apartments and youngsters dressed in Western style in the cities.

A Danube River harbor at Tulcea

A BALKAN COUNTRY

Romania is a Balkan country of 91,700 square miles (237,500 square kilometers). It reaches from the Black Sea and Moldova on the east across the Transylvanian Alps and the Carpathian mountains to the borders of Hungary and Yugoslavia on the west. Its oval shape extends for a distance of 320 miles (515 kilometers) from north to south and 450 miles (724 kilometers) from east to west. The Danube River forms a natural boundary flowing west to east along Romania's southern border with Bulgaria. The Prut River is a natural eastern border between Romania and Moldova. It empties into the Danube and then into the Black Sea. The country is almost equally divided between mountains and plains, hills and plateaus.

MOUNTAINS

The Carpathian mountain system is a great horseshoe-shaped range that surrounds the Transylvanian Plateau. The average

Left: The Transylvanian Alps near Braşov
Right: Traffic must wait while sheep are led across the road.

altitude of the plateau is 1,500 feet (457 meters). The Muresul River divides the plateau across its center and flows west into Hungary. The Carpathians are not very high. Most of them range from 3,000 to 6,000 feet (914 to 1,829 meters) in altitude and are easily crossed.

Near the center of the country are the Transylvanian Alps. They contain Romania's highest peak, Mt. Moldoveanu, at 8,343 feet (2,543 meters). Other mountains reaching 7,000 and 8,000 feet (2,134 and 2,438 meters) are favorite places for winter skiers and summertime hikers. High in the mountains are glacial lakes where the water temperature never gets above freezing and snow covers some peaks until midsummer. The slopes are heavily forested and provide homes for many kinds of wildlife. Foxes, deer, wolves, wild boars, lynx, bears, and martens roam freely. Higher up on these slopes, the land has been cleared for farming and sheep grazing. It is not unusual for auto and truck traffic to be delayed on some mountain roads while shepherds leisurely lead their sheep across them.

Bran Castle, the castle of the legendary Dracula

RIVERS AND LAKES

The mountains are the source of many rivers that meander through the country. The Muresul travels the country for 446 miles (718 kilometers), and the Prut River is 437 miles (703 kilometers) in length. The Danube, which originates in the Black Forest of Germany, flows through more than 600 miles (966 kilometers) of Romania. The Danube provides the countryside with water for its farmlands. At its mouth it forms a strikingly beautiful delta, teeming with wildlife, as it empties into the Black Sea.

The small lakes of Romania, numbering almost twenty-five thousand, add special beauty to the region. The largest, Lake Razim, is 152 square miles (394 square kilometers).

Romania's five major regions are Transylvania, Banat and Oltenia, Moldavia and Bukovina, Dobrogea, and Wallachia. They vary in terrain and natural resources as well as in local customs.

TRANSYLVANIA

Transylvania has long been known for its storybook castles and turbulent history. The legendary Dracula built a castle high in the mountains near the present city of Bistriţa. Today the region is tranquil. The rumble of Dracula's carriage wheels and the screams of imagined vampires are gone, but much romance remains. Castles, costumed peasants, sleepy villages, and modern cities are all a part of the Transylvanian landscape. They are set against a background of spectacular scenery—mountains and gorges, lush rolling foothills, rushing rivers, and gentle streams.

Some districts still keep the same customs, live according to the

Left: Romanian pottery Right: The Folk Art Museum in Bucharest

old legends, and produce the same kind of folk art their ancestors did. In a mountain district near the city of Braşov, one custom that survives relates to unwed, but marriageable, maidens. A tall fir tree stands in front of any household in which a young lady who is available for marriage resides. The bark is peeled off the tree and a wreath of dried flowers is attached to a cross near its top. Thus are the homes of these ladies "in waiting" readily identified by anyone traveling through the town.

Another Transylvanian custom is the *draica*, when men dress as women and, carrying flags and swords, perform an ancient dance. They dance in front of a church as a plea for a good harvest. The beat gets faster and faster so the perspiration streams down the dancers' faces to wet the ground. Perspiration is a symbol of rain, which nourishes the fields.

Transylvania was the center of the Dacian Kingdom until A.D. 106, when it was conquered by the Romans. It was the crossroads of European-Near East land routes, and was alternately occupied by Ottomans (Turks), Hungarians, and Saxons, as well as by Huns and Tatars. Its most persistent invaders from the fourteenth to the nineteenth centuries were the Turks. Romanians had always been unhappy with the incorporation of Transylvania into the Austria-Hungarian Empire, and they fought for the unity of their homeland. In December 1918, Transylvania, a historical province inhabited in majority by Romanians, became part of the Romanian Kingdom. Later, in September 1940, the northern part of Transylvania was annexed by Hungary, but it was returned to Romania after World War II.

To the north, Transylvania borders on Hungary. This area has been alternately controlled by Hungary and Romania for centuries. After World War II, when it was returned to Romania, there were still important concentrations of people of Hungarian and German origin, but the main ethnic group was the Romanians. Most of these people retain their original life-style and language.

Just a mile or two from the Ukraine border is a region known as Maramures, one of the most colorful areas of the country. It is rich in peasant culture; traditional peasant dress is a part of everyday life here.

Maramures is renowned for its many wooden churches, some dating back to 1642. They are put together with nothing more than wooden pegs, and some still retain their original frescoes.

In this region is the Wooden Spoon Museum, a private collection of Ioan Tugui, containing over five thousand spoons made of a hundred different kinds of wood from every corner of Romania and many parts of the world. Some are for use, some are merely decorative, and many are both functional and decorative. They range from the eighteenth century to a modern spoon from New York, which bears the inscription, "Kissin' don't last, cookin' do."

Here, too, in the village of Sapinta, is the Merry Cemetery, an unusual and whimsical creation of a man named Stan Patras. Each grave has a hand-carved memorial in pictures and words that relates to the life of the departed who rests underneath. Patras' house is now a museum. Since his death in 1977, his work has been carried on by one of his students.

BANAT AND OLTENIA

Between Transylvania and Wallachia lie the areas known as Banat and Oltenia, although they are usually thought of as part of Transylvania and Wallachia. They border Hungary and Yugoslavia and bear the same scars of invasions, migrations, and occupations as the rest of the country. These areas were in the path of the tribes who fought their way through or stayed in hopes of gaining control of those people already there. The region was plundered, subjugated under Turkish rule, and was, at various times, the home of Hungarians, Germans (Swabians), Serbs, and, predominantly and permanently, Romanians.

To the west, the Danube flows between Yugoslavia and Romania. The Danube enters Romania from Yugoslavia near the town of Turnu-Severin to begin its 600-mile (966-kilometer) journey along the border with Bulgaria to the Black Sea.

South of Turnu-Severin, the Danube flows through the thick forests and deep gorges of the Carpathians. The best known, the Cazanne Gorges, have provided a natural passage for trade, military invasions, and migrations from earliest times. It was through these gorges that Emperor Trajan and his troops crossed

The Iron Gates hydroelectric station

the Danube to conquer Dacia in A.D. 106. On each side of the riverbank are the ruins of a gigantic bridge built by Trajan's architect, Apollodor of Damascus, which allowed Trajan to reach Dacia.

Yugoslavia and Romania cooperated in building the Iron Gates hydroelectric station nearby between Turnu-Severin and Moldova Veche. The first station was finished in 1972 and construction began on a second. Dams, locks, and generating stations help control flooding and aid in river navigation. This power station greatly increases electric power to both countries.

Today Turnu-Severin is a busy river port. Steamers, tankers, barges, and patrol boats from neighboring countries form a constant stream of activity and attest to the fact that the Danube is indeed a main artery of commerce in the region.

Most of Romania has thermal springs. Baile Herculane is one of the most beautiful and popular spas, and lies north of Turnu-Severin. It boasts a climate so temperate that lilacs sometimes bloom twice a year. Located in the valley of the Cerna, it is protected from the snowstorms of the Wallachian plains and the wet Adriatic winds that blow across Yugoslavia. Vegetation is lush and wild on the hillsides.

Romanians consider their health very important and thoroughly enjoy the offerings of the magnificent spas like Baile

Mud baths at a health spa

Herculane and others. The mud baths, high in mineral content, are thought to have healing powers and are equally attractive to the well and unwell, Romanians and foreigners.

Struggle for this fertile area continued until it was resolved by the Paris Peace Treaty in 1919. The eastern one-third was awarded to Romania, while the new kingdom of Yugoslavia divided the rest with Hungary.

MOLDAVIA AND BUKOVINA

In the late thirteenth century, a feudal state called Moldavia was established. It was ruled by a prince surrounded by his officials and boyars (landlords), who were served by a small group of freemen and a large number of serfs.

In the fifteenth and sixteenth centuries, Stephan the Great, Prince of Moldavia, defender of Christianity, and his son Petru Rares, built a ring of fortifications from Suceava, which was then the capital, to the Danube port of Galaţi. Stephan turned the area into a forward defense line against the Turks, with whom he waged endless battles.

Religious and historical paintings, once a source of education for the peasants, still cover the exterior walls of this monastery.

One of the most unusual cultures in Europe developed behind this ring of fortifications. It consisted of a series of distinctive painted monasteries that combined traditional folk art with Byzantine and Gothic influences. A new school of painters covered the monastery walls, outside as well as inside, with colorful and imaginative biblical and historical scenes. The paintings served as a source of education for the local peasantry, who had no other educational opportunities. Today the colors in these frescoes remain vivid, but the secret of how they were done died with the unknown artists who painted them.

Harvesting onions

Rich tapestries, embroidered hangings and altar cloths, silver bookbindings, goblets and candlesticks, and unusually artistic icons (religious paintings on wood or metal) are among the treasures displayed within the monasteries.

Suceava flourished as a trade center under Stephan's rule, but like other cities of the region, eventually fell into decay. Recently it has been revitalized. Today it is an important industrial center and boasts one of the largest steel plants in Europe.

Mile upon mile of Moldavian roads are lined on both sides with walnut trees. In the shade of the trees, peasants pause for lunch, or for a snack of walnuts, to rest from their labors in the fields with scythes, spades, rakes, and hoes. The reality of farming methods differs greatly from the giant combines and harvesters once pictured on TV, with proud overseers of the collectives telling the audience how well the harvest is going with all those modern machines.

*The Bicaz
Gorge area*

Moldavia and a small area of villages in the north, known as Bukovina, have Ukraine as their neighbor. The Prut River divides the two countries and flows south to Galaţi, the southernmost point in Moldavia and a major river port. The Siretul River runs almost parallel to the Prut to the west. The two rivers meet at the Danube near Galaţi.

In the picturesque valley formed by the Bistriţa River is the Bicaz Gorge. A river 5 yards (4.5 meters) wide cuts through the 1,000-foot (305-meter) high gorge. Sunlight hardly penetrates, and

Pastel floral patterns decorate a farmhouse.

even the weeds turn yellow. It is an awe-inspiring sight. But the city of Bicaz nearby is shrouded in cement dust from the industry that surrounds it.

In the Bistriţa valley, too, is a mountain resort called Red Lake. It reflects the glow from the red granite mountains that tower around it. The lake was formed by a landslide into the valley that engulfed many small lakes. From the surface of the lake emerge the tops of fir trees that once covered the mountainsides.

Farming and timber communities in the region appear unchanged since earlier times. Thatch-roofed cottages, pastel-colored houses painted with floral patterns, costumed peasants, and gardens bursting with blooms compose a picture in which time seems to have stood still.

Left: The entrance to a farmhouse   Right: The rich, flat lands of Dobrogea are used for growing crops.

Between the Siretul and Prut rivers farther south is a pleasant rolling plateau that reaches to the region where Moldavia, Wallachia, and Dobrogea meet the Danube.

DOBROGEA

Between the Danube River and the Black Sea in eastern Romania lies a small plain known as Dobrogea. It is the flattest land in Romania. Flourishing vineyards, some farmland, and a variety of historical sights make up the western portion of the area. The lower two-thirds of the Black Sea coast is lined with white, sandy beaches and an increasing number of modern resort facilities and spas. It is known as the Romanian Riviera and is an important tourist attraction.

The northern third of Dobrogea encompasses the Danube Delta. The delta covers almost 2,000 miles (3,219 kilometers) of marshes, reed beds, dense forests overgrown with vines, small lakes and waterways, and remote fishing villages. It contains one of

A part of the Danube Delta

Europe's leading wildlife sanctuaries. Hundreds of varieties of migratory birds from every corner of the globe use the area for a stopping place. Here the Danube branches out into the Chilia, Sulina, and Sfîntul-Gheorghe rivers to create an ever-changing wonderland. Fishing is an important industry here; the prize catches are the large sturgeon, which are the source of excellent Romanian caviar.

As a province of the Roman Empire until A.D. 271, Dobrogea was linked to the rest of Europe not only by the Danube and the long sea route, but by a road that entered Dacia by way of Turnu-Severin, the site of the Iron Gates. Dobrogea was the path of the many legions who roamed the area.

The Black Sea was an important trade route during ancient times, and there were constant barbarian invasions in successive attempts to dominate the area. Each civilization left behind something of its own culture. But eventually Dobrogea was reduced to an overgrown area of rubble until the late nineteenth century. Romanian aristocracy recognized the advantages of its long, warm summers and began building villas and chalets along the coast.

Plains of Wallachia

As excavations continue for new hotels and housing, the entire region has become an archaeologist's paradise. Bulldozers dig deeper and deeper and find more and more antiquities. Mosques and museums hold a treasure trove of the past.

WALLACHIA

Wallachia covers the entire width of southern Romania. Most of the area consists of plains, including the vast fertile lands created by the Danube. With the Danube now controlled by the Iron Gates systems of locks and dams, corn, sunflowers, wheat, and other grains grow in abundance.

The foothills of the Carpathians border on "Old Wallachia," where farms, vineyards, and orchards blanket the valleys. The industrialization of nearby areas has not destroyed its natural beauty. Throughout the valleys of the Oltul and Jiu rivers are resorts and spas, villas and hamlets, and pastoral scenery along country roads.

The Dîmbovita River divides Wallachia and flows through Romania's capital city, Bucharest.

Chapter 2

FORMING A NATION

DACIANS

Romania has had twenty-two centuries of dramatic and violent history. Although archaeological excavations reveal traces of habitation since the Paleolithic Age, the first inhabitants who actually settled here were the Dacians, who appeared in about 200 B.C. and named the region "Dacia." The Dacians were a culturally advanced tribe from the Balkan region, and for about three hundred years lived there in peace, farming, mining gold and iron ore, and trading with neighboring tribes. They enjoyed advances in music, astronomy, and medicine. They were ruled by kings, who in turn were advised by high priests.

DACO-ROMAN CIVILIZATION

Decebal, king of the Dacians, had managed to resist two previous attempts to conquer the area by Roman emperors, Domitian and Nerva. Then Emperor Trajan and his legions

Opposite page: Roman ruins in Dobrogea on the Black Sea

Left: Roman Emperor Trajan   Right: Vlad Tepes

invaded and finally conquered Dacia in A.D. 106 and made it a province of the Roman Empire. Then came a period of great colonization and a blending of cultures to form a Daco-Roman civilization. The region became the most Romanized of all the empire's colonies.

Roman influence continued even after Rome officially withdrew from the region in A.D. 275. A large number of colonists stayed on and retained their language and Roman ways. The region became a "Latin island" despite continued invasions by other tribes and nations. These colonists, who refused to assimilate with their conquerors, were the ancestors of today's Romanians.

INVASIONS AND FEUDAL STATES

For five hundred years after the Romans withdrew, the area suffered countless invasions by barbarian tribes. The invaders included Bulgars, Goths, Huns, Magyars, Slavs, and Tatars. These groups intermarried with the Romanians, who nonetheless continued to keep their cultural identity.

Small political units were formed gradually during the tenth and eleventh centuries. Moldavia became a feudal state in the late thirteenth century. Also in the thirteenth century, Wallachia came into being as a feudal principality. Among the most famous Wallachian princes was Mircea the Old, who managed to defeat the Turkish invaders under Baiazid Ilderim. His heroic struggles were evoked by Romanian poets and historians.

Another famous feudal prince was Vlad Tepes or Vlad the Impaler, who was also known as Count Dracula, whose ruthlessness contributed to the emergence of the myth of Dracula. He was, however, a staunch defender of his country's independence. He organized armed resistance against Turkish invaders. He ruled from 1456 to 1462.

The prince's family name was Dracul, meaning "dragon" or "devil," and he assumed the name Dracula, which means "son of the devil." It was Dracula's method of treating his enemies that earned him the name Vlad the Impaler. Legend has it that he murdered twenty thousand of the enemy by impaling them on spears or sharp stakes, there to suffer slow and painful deaths.

More tales of his atrocities depict him as a sadistic tyrant and a bloodthirsty monster. Superstition gave rise to the belief that Vlad Tepes was a vampire. But this was really a figment of the imagination of the nineteenth-century Irish novelist, Bram Stoker.

Stoker's horror story of the "Un-dead" vampire Count Dracula was published in 1897. *Nosferatu* is the Eastern European term for "Un-dead." Dozens of books and films have followed with themes similar to Stoker's Gothic depiction of the struggle between good and evil.

Dracula's castle was described by Stoker as being "on the wall of a terrible precipice. A stone falling from the window would fall a thousand feet without touching anything. As far as the eye can reach is a sea of green tree-tops, with occasionally a deep rift where there is a chasm." His tale leads from this eerie spot high in the Transylvanian Alps to London and back where Dracula was finally put to death in true vampire fashion. His head was cut off, a stake was driven through his heart, his mouth was filled with garlic, and he disappeared in a cloud of dust.

Dracula's death occurred in 1476. By the end of the 1500s, the Turks had a firm grasp on the area. Then the warrior Michael the Brave, a Romanian hero, appeared on the scene and briefly united the three principalities of Moldavia, Wallachia, and Transylvania for the first time in 1601. But the Turks reclaimed Wallachia, Poland invaded Moldavia, and Hungary retook Transylvania.

While the Turks were occupying the area, the Germans and Hungarians also moved into Transylvania. In spite of all these invasions, the Romanians remained in the majority. None of the invaders managed to gain full control, but neither were the Romanians able to develop as a unified state because of their preoccupation with fighting off the incursions.

UNIFICATION

Political unification of the area now known as Romania began between 1250 and 1350, when the people of Wallachia joined to form a single state under one ruler. The people of Moldavia did the same shortly after. Each state was ruled by a prince, and was called a "principality." The three Romanian principalities were first united in 1601 by Michael the Brave. Though short-lived, this unification contributed to the strengthening of Romanian national identity.

The independence of the principalities did not last long. The Ottoman Empire imposed its rule over the Danubian Principalities in spite of strong Romanian resistance. The Romanians were under Turkish domination for almost three hundred years, although the Turks allowed the Romanians some native rulers, and the type of control was less cruel and less effective than in other Turkish-occupied countries.

CONSTANTIN BRANCOVEANU

During this period, a Romanian prince named Constantin Brancoveanu ruled Wallachia for seventeen years. He was instrumental in bringing about many cultural changes, including a new style of architecture known as Brancovan. It was a blending of Renaissance and Byzantine styles with Romanian folk tradition. When Brancoveanu fell out of favor with the Turks in 1714, he and his four sons were taken to Constantinople and executed.

PHANARIOTS

Later in the eighteenth century, Moldavia and Wallachia joined forces with Russia and Austria to fight the Turks. To insure against defeat and fortify their authority, the Turks sold the two principalities to Greek merchants known as Phanariots. They were cruel owners who were only interested in reaping profits from the area. The lowly peasant, already oppressed by high taxes and hard work, was now forced to produce for his Phanariot master as well as pay taxes to the sultan, the prince, and the boyar.

TURKS AND RUSSIANS

During this time, Moldavia and Wallachia were the scenes of many fierce battles between the Russians and the Turks fighting for possession of the area. The peasants finally revolted against these harsh rulers. Between 1829 and 1878, the Turkish Empire lost more and more of its territories because of its continuing wars with Russia and the struggle for national independence in the occupied territories. In 1878, Turkish influence over Romania came to an end.

The elastic borders of Romania were reshaped once more by the Russians. The peace settlement returned Bessarabia to Russia, and Romania finally acquired an outlet to the Black Sea in northern Dobrogea. Bessarabia is the often-disputed section of northeastern Moldavia between the Prut and Dniester rivers. Known as the Moldavian Socialist Republic under Ceausescu, it had been shuttled between Russia and Romania for more than one hundred years. It is a Romanian historical province currently seeking reunification with Romania, despite ongoing ethnic disputes.

After the Turks were defeated in a war with the tzarist empire, Russia drew up a constitution in 1829 for the Romanian principalities that gave power to a group of noblemen. In 1834, Russia withdrew from Romania and representative government began. In 1859, Wallachia and Moldavia united to form a single nation under one ruler. Prince Alexander John Cuza was elected as the first ruler of Romania.

FIRST RULERS OF ROMANIA

Once Wallachia and Moldavia were unified, young Romanians demanded many reforms. They called for improved living

A sketch of a Wallachian village from 1877 (left) and King Carol I

conditions for the underprivileged and fairer representation for
the peasants. Prince Cuza heeded their demands by having the
government buy land from the wealthy Romanians to give to the
peasants. Cuza's government also built more free schools for the
poor.

But Cuza's measures antagonized some members of the
Romanian elite, and the prince was forced to resign in 1866.
Influential Romanian politicians chose Karl of Hohenzollern, a
German prince, to take over the rule of Romania.

In the same year, the major countries of Europe officially
recognized Romania as an independent nation. In 1881, Romania
became a kingdom. Karl, who had Latinized his name to Prince
Carol, became King Carol I and ruled for over thirty years.

Chapter 3

THE TWENTIETH CENTURY

KING CAROL I

Under the rule of King Carol I, Romania's first political parties developed. The people were given the right to elect their own government representatives, but the electoral system was complicated and full of obstacles that kept the peasants from having any influence over how their country was run. Romania's economy grew under King Carol I, but the rich became richer and the peasants gained little that improved the quality of their lives.

In 1907, the peasants again revolted. Buildings and houses were burned. Crops were destroyed and many landowners suffered economically. The Romanian army killed ten thousand peasants before the revolt was finally stopped.

WORLD WAR I

World War I began in 1914, the year King Carol I died. Carol was succeeded on the throne by his nephew, Ferdinand. Ferdinand was married to Marie, granddaughter of Queen Victoria of Great Britain. Through her efforts, Ferdinand was

King Ferdinand

persuaded to remain neutral at the beginning of World War I. Then in 1916 Romania joined France, Great Britain, and their Allies in the battle against the Central Powers, mainly Austria-Hungary and Germany.

The Allies defeated the Central Powers and, as part of its reward for being on the victorious side, Romania was given the provinces that had belonged to Austria-Hungary: Banat, Bukovina, and Transylvania. These territories had large Romanian populations and easily melded into the rest of Romania. With the acquisition of the new territories, Romania almost doubled in size and population. Now, for the first time in its long and troubled history, Romanian lands included almost all of the Romanian people and marked the boundaries of the country as it is today.

BEGINNINGS OF FASCISM AND COMMUNISM

Despite the efforts of King Ferdinand to institute much-needed land reforms in Romania, the old feudal system held fast. There were extremes of wealth and poverty. After Ferdinand's death in

*Left: Michael and his father King Carol II watch a military ceremony
in 1930. Right: A German and a Romanian share guard duty in 1941.*

1927, King Carol II and Carol's young son Michael alternated
ruling the country. In Romania, as in all of Europe, there were
depressions and severe economic hardships. In desperation, many
Romanians turned to fascism or communism.

A Fascist group known as the Iron Guard wanted to take over
power, but was defeated by the army under General Ion
Antonescu. To regain its historical territories confiscated by the
Soviet Union in 1940, Antonescu's government developed an
alliance with Nazi Germany.

WORLD WAR II

Meanwhile, in 1940, Hungary occupied Transylvania. Romania
was forced to enter World War II on the side of Germany, but
fought a losing battle as USSR pushed farther into the country.

King Michael finally succeeded in ousting the pro-German government and Romania joined the Allies on August 23, 1944. In the post-war settlement, Romania regained Transylvania.

ROMANIA BECOMES A PEOPLE'S REPUBLIC

With the Soviets in the country as head of the Allied Control Council to assist in the reorganization of the war-torn land, the tiny Communist party easily rigged elections and took over power. King Michael was forced to step down in December 1947, and Romania was proclaimed a people's republic.

Romania's government, educational system, and economy were reorganized according to Communist principles, and the nation became a Soviet satellite. Since foreign policy also was controlled by the Soviets, Romania's national interest was made subordinate to that of the USSR. Many Romanians were dissatisfied with the Soviet interference that continued in their affairs.

GHEORGHIU-DEJ, GENERAL SECRETARY

By the early 1960s, the once small Romanian Communist party was exerting full control over Romanian society. Romanian leaders wanted to establish support from the population. Gheorghe Gheorghiu-Dej, who had been leader of the party since 1945, was the man responsible for the harsh Stalinist policies of the 1950s. Gheorghiu-Dej was the general secretary of the party and the chief of state until his death in March 1965. In the early 1960s, he engaged in a less pro-Soviet orientation and challenged Soviet tutelage over Romania.

Toward the end of his tenure, Gheorghiu-Dej worked for his

severe economic policies, more emphasis on consumer goods, and more independence for Romania, although still within the guidelines of Marxist-Leninist dogma.

A NEW CONSTITUTION AND A NEW LEADER

A new constitution was adopted in 1965, which stressed the country's control over its own affairs. It was in that year that Nicolae Ceausescu became president and changed the name of the country to the Socialist Republic of Romania. Ceausescu, a peasant's son, had become active in the Communist party when he was very young. He was arrested as a revolutionary and spent the late 1930s and early 1940s in jail, where he became friendly with Gheorghiu-Dej. After they both escaped in 1944, Ceausescu held numerous posts within the party, while Gheorghiu-Dej was first secretary. Ceausescu inherited the post of party head when Gheorghiu-Dej died.

The Ceausescu ancestral home is in the village of Scornicesti, and the whole area was once a monument to this ruler. Formerly a poor peasant village, Scornicesti soon boasted paved streets, a soccer stadium, discotheque, candy factory and stores stocked with goods not usually found in most villages.

Opposite the completely renovated cottage where Ceausescu was born stood a stone monument, and on a hillside close to the marble tombs of Ceausescu's parents there was a new, small Orthodox church.

Ceausescu may possibly have been one of the most powerful leaders Romania will ever have. He developed his own Marxist dictatorship. But his promises of economic improvement were not fulfilled, and Romania continued to face dramatic economic

*In 1970, President Pompidou of France (fourth from left)
entertained President and Mrs. Ceausescu (on either side of
Pompidou) at a theater presentation in Paris.*

crisis. Promised foodstuffs and consumer goods were difficult to
get. Customarily, people had to wait in long lines to buy goods,
becoming more embittered each time, as supplies were often gone
before they reached the counter.

The Western media abundantly described the ordeal of
Romanians under President Ceausescu's regime. The country was
ruled by the president himself, and his wife, Elena, was his main
adviser and associate. Of the many positions she held, the most
important was that of personnel director of the Central Committee.
Since her husband often shifted blame for errors or failures to
subordinates, Elena was kept busy "rearranging" top-echelon
people and jobs in both the party and government leaderships.
Even if Ceausescu were training her to possibly take over the
government at some time, she would not have lasted long, being
deeply disliked by the people. Ceausescu and his wife were the
main beneficiaries of the Romanian riches, and transformed the
former royal castle in Sinaia into a special family residence.

Speaking at a rally in August 1968, Nicolae Ceausescu
demanded the withdrawal of Soviet troops from Czechoslovakia.

A FAMILY AFFAIR

It is said that at least forty members of the Ceausescus' families had positions of authority in this government. This distribution of power was possibly laying the foundation for a dynasty.

Daughter Zora Elena was director of the Mathematical Institute. Nicu, their son, might have been under consideration as Ceausescu's successor when he was put in charge of the Communist Youth Union, along with several other important positions. However, his sense of responsibility was obviously lacking as it became apparent that he appeared more interested in liquor, women and fast flashy cars.

FOREIGN RELATIONS

In 1964, Romania exchanged ambassadors with the United States and in 1969 hosted the state visit of President Richard Nixon. Romania chose to remain neutral in the dispute between the Soviets and China, but the real test of Romania's independent thinking came at the time of the Soviet invasion of Czechoslovakia in August 1968.

Huge crowds of Ceausescu's countrymen gathered to hear him speak out against the invasion and in favor of Soviet noninterference in the internal affairs of other nations. He restated his belief in the right of self-rule and refused to send his soldiers to aid the USSR in its dealings with Czechoslovakia. One week later, however, Ceausescu backed down and proclaimed friendship with the USSR. He was a loyal partner of the Soviet Union in the Warsaw Pact alliance.

Still, there were important signs of Romania's relative independence; no Soviet bases were allowed within the borders of the country, nor had Romania participated in Warsaw Pact maneuvers since 1962. Ceausescu also defied the Warsaw Pact countries by sending Romanian athletes to compete in the 1984 Olympics in Los Angeles while the rest of the Eastern European countries boycotted the events.

THE GOVERNMENT

Romania had a single-party political system under the official name, the Congress of the Romanian Communist Party. Nicolae Ceausescu was General Secretary of the party, as well as being President of the Socialist Democracy and Unity Front, Chairman of the Council of State (a permanent body composed of 28 members with power to issue decrees, all enforceable as law) and the President of the Socialist Republic of Romania.

Ceausescu's government maintained an extensive system of restrictions on the lives of Romanians. During anti-government demonstrations in 1989, government forces killed hundreds.

*The former Communist headquarters (left) and a meeting of
the Communist Party Congress (right) in Bucharest*

Protests spread across Romania and, in Bucharest, thousands
were killed when government security forces fired on
demonstrating crowds who were demanding the resignation of
Ceausescu. Military forces joined in the revolt against security
forces. Ceausescu and his wife fled Bucharest on December 22, but
were captured. At a secret trial they were charged with murder
and embezzlement of government funds, found guilty, and
executed on December 25, 1989. Most of Ceausescu's family and
followers were sentenced to long prison terms. The National
Salvation Front, a group made up chiefly of former Communist
party members, took control. Ion Iliescu, leader of the Front,
became acting president of Romania. At free multiparty elections
in 1990 and 1992 Iliescu won the presidency.

From that time, Romania has begun a troubled movement
toward democratic reforms. A nationwide referendum
overwhelmingly endorsed a new Constitution on December 8,
1991. Guarantees for free speech, pluralism, human rights, privacy
and the protection of private property are provided.

The new Constitution defines Romania as a republic where the
law prevails in a social and democratic state. Private property

rights and a market economy are guaranteed. The head of the state is the president elected by direct vote for a maximum of two four-year terms. After election, the president may not belong to a political party. The bicameral parliament consists of an upper house, the Senate, and a lower house, the Chamber of Deputies, both elected for four-year terms. The Supreme Court of Justice is the "defender of the people." Justices are nominated to six-year terms by the president but subject to the approval of Parliament. A system of district and local judges exists below the Supreme Court.

Romania is the first Soviet-bloc country to have outlawed its Communist party. The party was nearly destroyed by the revolt of 1989 when the new government seized its assets and many followers renounced membership. However, it was not fully disbanded and was reborn in November 1990 as the Socialist Labor Party.

The free-market economy reforms of the new government eventually resulted in higher prices, increasing inflation and demonstrations for higher wages and removal of the government.

THE ECONOMY AND THE CULT OF CEAUSESCU

One could say that the economy and cult of Ceausescu were the cause of his downfall. By the mid-1980s, as debt piled up and unneeded building projects moved forward, the living standard for the average Romanian had dropped 20 to 30 percent. The vast amounts of money spent on industrialization and monumental projects severely curtailed personal improvements to living. Money that might have been spent to modernize farming methods

An officially staged demonstration on behalf of Ceausescu and his clan

and make consumer products available was being poured into
projects to insure that the name of Ceausescu would have a place
in history alongside Mircea the Old, Stephan the Great, and
Michael the Brave—heroes all.

Ceausescu's legacy includes the creation of gigantic steel and
aluminum industries that could be utilized at only half capacity
because there was no market for their products.

Then there was the new government center in the middle of
Bucharest, planned as a "Palace of the Republic," with an open
plaza to hold 500,000 people. One can only guess that Ceausescu
envisioned it accommodating that many of his cheering and
adoring countrymen. To initiate this project, hundreds of
buildings, old and new, were razed, including twelve historic
churches and three synagogues. Forty thousand people would be
evicted from apartments and homes with the cost of the project
estimated at 1.2 billion dollars.

Already finished was a canal between the Danube and the Black
Sea. It is hardly used. In process was a 1.8 billion-dollar irrigation
system. But to the dismay of environmentalists, the government

Browsing at a bookstall in Bucharest

came up with a plan to fill in much of the Danube Delta wetlands to create new farmlands.

At one time the history museum in Tirgoviste featured an exhibit of prominent Romanians. Of course, Ceausescu's immense portrait was included, gazing down on busts of Romania's rulers, among whom was Vlad Dracula. Around the entrance to the museum were also the large busts of Decebal, the Dacian king and Trajan, the Roman emperor who defeated Decebal in the second century. Ceausescu was a part of this history.

It was not likely that Romanians could easily forget who was ruling the country. Bookstores were required to devote entire showcases to the twenty-eight volumes of Ceausescu's speeches. Newsstands had to display volumes also, but not all of them. Music stores sold records of his speeches. Artists and writers produced works celebrating his accomplishments. Ceausescu had the entrance to the Bucharest Fairground framed by a new triumphal arch bearing the legend "The Golden Epoch—the Epoch of Nicolae Ceausescu." Even high-ranking officials were required to rise to their feet at party functions and chant, "Ceausescu—Romania, our pride and esteem."

Bucharest, the capital and largest city of Romania

Bucharest
★

Chapter 4

A REGIONAL TOUR

The personalities of Romania's cities are as diverse as the lands they occupy. Customs and costumes vary according to the origins of the previous settlers and conquerors. Each city has its cultural traditions but each adheres to the wave of nationalism that is bringing them into the modern world.

BUCHAREST

The pulse of Romania, quite naturally, is Bucharest, the largest city and the capital since 1861. It lies near the center of Wallachia and is the region's main attraction. Nearly two million people live there. Although pre-World War I architecture remains in some of the old sections of the city, most of it is modern, with clean, white, functional buildings lining wide avenues. It is spacious and sprawling and, during the summer months, green and flowering. A small Triumphal Arch was built in 1922 to commemorate Romania's heroes who died in World War I. Bucharest has terrace restaurants, sidewalk cafes, and some French-influenced architecture. All these attributes earned Bucharest the name "Paris of the Balkans."

There are no records to check, but the city probably dates back to the fourteenth century, when it was a military fortress and trade center on the route between Central Europe and Constantinople.

According to legend, the city was named after Bucur, a shepherd who settled there. The Bucar Church in the city is believed to stand in his memory. Its tower roof is shaped like a shepherd's cap. The first known mention of the site as "Bucharest" was made by Vlad the Impaler in 1459. He built a fortress there on the Dîmbovita River as part of a network of defenses against the Turks. It became the residence of several Wallachian princes. In 1698, Bucharest became the capital of Wallachia under Prince Brancoveanu. After Moldavia and Wallachia were united in 1861, it was made the capital of Romania.

Most of the city had to be rebuilt repeatedly. It was ravaged by fires, invasions, earthquakes, and occupations throughout the centuries. Bucharest has been known as an up-to-date city bustling with industry and culture. Vestiges of the past are visible in its Byzantine, Turkish, and old Romanian structures that stand side by side with the modern skyscrapers. One of the oldest structures is the fifteenth-century Princely Court, which is now a museum. Unfortunately, the Communist party demolished many valuable historical monuments. Churches and synagogues were bulldozed for other projects, despite the general protest of Romanian intellectuals.

As the look of Bucharest changed from past to present, its

New apartment buildings overlook old housing (above) and both new and old automobiles make up the traffic in the central area of Bucharest (below).

Above: An old section of central Bucharest
Below: Soviet architecture of the Scinteii House (left)
and the neoclassical Athenaeum (right)

Two Brancovan style churches built in the eighteenth century, Stavropoleos (left) and Cretulescu (right)

architecture changed to elaborate "wedding-cake Russian" and Western functional. It is a clean city. No trash litters the streets or parks. There are no billboards. A new subway system was under construction with two lines already in operation.

Old churches in the Brancovan style, such as Stavropoleos and Cretulescu from the seventeenth and eighteenth centuries, are nestled among new, deluxe hotels, libraries, theaters, and museums. There is an old university (1864) and there is a new university area (1935); the Athenaeum, a neoclassical concert hall with beautiful gardens; and Scinteii House, the nation's largest publishing institution.

Editorial offices for everything relating to the written word are contained in Scinteii House, a gigantic complex of buildings. It was the headquarters of the Ministry of Culture (the Council for Socialist Culture and Education), which controlled all publications. Within its confines is the country's largest printing

Two views of the Museum of the Village and Folk Art, which contains over three hundred peasant houses and outbuildings arranged according to regions

plant, which printed the daily Communist newspaper, *Scinteia (The Spark)*, the organ of the party's Central Committee. About 490 papers and magazines, including regional and ethnic, are now published countrywide. The 1991 constitution abolished censorship.

An outstanding attraction in the heart of Bucharest is the Museum of the Village and Folk Art, a "city" in the middle of Herastrau Park. Some of its structures are over three hundred years old. These buildings were carefully taken apart at their original sites and brought to the park piece by piece. Skilled craftsmen from each village reassembled them. The reconstructed village is complete with lawns, flowers, paths, and lanes leading to churches, wells, barns, homes, and wayside shrines. The buildings are filled with over 1,100 artifacts, including objects of folk art, tools, and household and religious items arranged to give visitors a keen sense of Romania's rich past.

Ploiești oil fields

On the shores of Lake Snagov, a few miles from Bucharest, stands a fifteenth-century chapel. The headless remains of Dracula are said to be buried in it. Dracula was thought to have been killed in one of his many battles with the Turks, who then carried his head off on a stake, as he had done to his Turkish foes. His conquerors displayed their trophy in Constantinople.

PLOIEȘTI

The oil fields and refineries of Ploiești are only a short distance from Bucharest. It was over a century ago that oil was discovered in this region. Thereafter, its derricks often lit the skies like giant Christmas trees. Its refineries processed most of the country's crude oil. The output was second only to that of the Soviet Union among the Communist Bloc countries.

Unfortunately, though, the market for these refined products shrank throughout the world. But Romania was tied to agreements to buy Soviet oil at world prices, refine it into gasoline and sell it abroad—at a loss. Soviet oil had to be paid for in hard

The town hall of Ploieşti

currency (money that has international trading value) or
Romanian goods that otherwise could have been sold in the West
for that much-needed currency.

All activity in the Ploieşti oil fields was interrupted during
World War II because the fields were an important source of oil
for Germany. It was a target of intense bombing by the Allied
Forces in the 1940s. The city and its industry have been almost
entirely rebuilt since then. One of the most interesting sights in
Ploieşti is the Republican Oil Museum, comparable to those seen
in Texas.

In spite of all Romania's refineries, gasoline was periodically
rationed. In 1992 oil production was approximately 6.61 million
tonnes and reserves are expected to be exhausted by the mid-
1990s. Crude oil has to be imported.

But all is not oil in Ploieşti. The Caragiale Museum here is
devoted to the life and works of Ion Caragiale, the noted
Romanian dramatist who died in 1912.

Peles Castle was a royal residence during the late nineteenth century.

SINAIA

In the seventeenth century, Mihail Cantacuzino built a monastery to commemorate his visit to Mt. Sinai. Around this monastery arose the Wallachian resort town of Sinaia, called the "Pearl of the Carpathians." The beauty of the area's alpine landscape lured many aristocrats there to build villas, including King Carol I, who built a summer home in 1875, called Peles Castle. The castle resembles the medieval castles of southern Germany, with its slim turrets, timber and plaster walls, and dormer windows that look down on sweeping lawns and gardens.

Nothing about this fairy-tale castle is Romanian except its location. It was first designed by a Viennese architect, continued by a German designer, and built by a Czech builder. Inside is a magnificent profusion of Italian Renaissance, German Baroque, French Rococo, Turkish, and Moorish styles. Wood dominates the

Beautiful carved wood in the interior of Peles Castle

interior. Heavily carved paneling, staircases, doors, ceilings, and cupboards are overwhelmingly elaborate. The former royal castle became a presidential residence reserved for Nicolae Ceausescu and his family.

Yesterday's villas are today's tourist accommodations. Skiers and hikers take advantage of the many cafes, restaurants, and entertainment facilities. Flower-lined promenades encourage visitors to wander through this peaceful city.

PREDEAL

Transylvania probably has more picturesque cities within its borders than any other region. Hungarians, Germans, and several other nationalities still inhabit the area along with the Romanians, and the customs of each are thoroughly intertwined.

One of the cities is Predeal, Romania's highest town, 3,500 feet (1,077 meters) above the Prahova and Timis rivers. It is the watershed that separates Wallachia from Transylvania. Near the

Bran Castle (left), built by merchants in the fourteenth century, and the village of Brașov (right)

city stands Bran Castle, one of the best examples of Gothic architecture in all of Europe. It was built by German merchants in the fourteenth century. German knights lived in it and collected tolls from travelers as they passed between Transylvania and Wallachia.

Bran Castle was home to Dracula during the time he was waiting to regain his title of Prince of Wallachia. He had held that title for a few months when he was seventeen years old. Twenty rooms of medieval art are on display there.

BRAȘOV

A little Romanian village tucked in the corner of the Transylvanian plateau called Brasovechi was occupied by Teutonic knights from Saxony in the twelfth century. It is said that a tree was uprooted and a golden crown was found at the site. So the name of the city was changed to Kronstadt, which

Above: Promenading, a favorite pastime in the early evening, is a social event.
Below: St. Nicholas Church (left) and the Black Church (right)

The tractor factory, adorned with a tractor sculpture (left), and a part of the old city

means "The Crown City." After World War II, as a goodwill gesture to the Russians, the name became Orasul Stalin. When Stalin went out of favor, the name of the city became Braşov.

Braşov, rumored to have been built by giants, is Romania's second city in both size and industry. Like most other Romanian cities, it is a combination of ancient and modern. The center of the "old city" has the reconstructed ruins of the largest Catholic church in the country, the Black Church, which was gutted by fire in the seventeenth century. The remaining smoke-blackened walls gave it its name. The interior is very austere, except for some beautiful oriental rugs.

The Orthodox church of St. Nicholas was built in the sixteenth century. Its clock tower was a gift of Empress Elizabeth of Russia in 1751. The walls inside are covered with primitive paintings and icons made of hammered gold. The first Romanian school was housed in the building's courtyard in 1595. Today the building is a museum.

Close to the old city stands the Tractor Factory, with rows of tractors standing ready for export.

Braşov is a bustling city filled with tourists eager to start their holidays in the nearby mountains.

A street light commemorates the fact that, in 1884, Timişoara was the first Romanian city to light its streets with electricity.

TIMIŞOARA

Timişoara, in the Banat area of Transylvania, became the center of engineering and textile industries, and a melting pot of cultures. It has Romanian, German, and Magyar (Hungarian) state theaters, a Serbian Dance Ensemble, and a Serbian newpaper. Its eighteenth-century architecture is famous throughout the Balkans. It is a river port city connected to the Danube by the Bega Canal. The canal begins in the center of the city and is lined with open-air cafes and docks for small boats. To the west of the city it widens to accommodate larger cargo carriers.

Timişoara has one of the country's largest universities, an opera house, and many fine museums. It is interesting to note that in 1884, Timişoara was the first city in Romania to use electricity for street lighting.

A Gothic Church on the Hill dominates Sighişoara.

SIGHIŞOARA

On the Transylvanian Plateau is the town of Sighişoara, resembling a medieval "burg." Small homes and cottages huddle around its citadel and monastery. A Gothic Church on the Hill can be reached by climbing a flight of 172 steps. It has a fourteenth-century clock with seven carved figures representing the days of the week. A mechanism in the tower sets these figures in motion as the clock runs. Cobblestone streets, a covered bridge, gabled houses, and lush, green terraces give the feeling of the Middle Ages.

Sibiu

SIBIU

German-Saxon merchants settled in the village of Cibinum in the twelfth century. They built a beautiful city, now known as Sibiu. From the thirteenth to the eighteenth centuries, the inhabitants suffered plagues, fires, and earthquakes, in addition to invasions by Turks and barbarians. They became convinced that witchcraft was the cause of so many disasters, and they reacted by systematically butchering hundreds who were suspect. They built deep moats around towers and bastions for protection. Moss-covered sections of these walls and moats remain as a reminder of a devastating past.

The present is truly lovely, however. The town is built on two levels. The sloping streets of both levels are connected by picturesque stairways. Lining the streets are old houses with

*An illuminated Bible in Brukenthal Museum
and a part of the old city wall in Sibiu*

red-tiled roofs and long, narrow windows. Gateways lead into mysterious byways in the old section.

Industrial plants that produce most of Romania's beer, automobiles, candy, furniture, canned goods, textiles, and leather surround the town. But these industries do not intrude on the charm of the old town.

One of the oldest and finest collections of ethnological, historical, and scientific objects is housed in the Brukenthal Museum of Sibiu. The museum was formerly the mansion of an eighteenth-century governor of Transylvania. Galleries of Romanian and European artworks enhance an already immense private collection. Rooms are filled with more than 200,000 books, some dating from the fifteenth and sixteenth centuries. The first Romanian book, incidentally, was printed in Sibiu in 1544.

IAŞI

Iaşi the former capital of Moldavia, lies on the plateau near Romania's eastern border with Moldova. In spite of invasions and plundering by Tatars, Turks, and Poles, much fifteenth- to nineteenth-century beauty remains. There are monasteries, a Palace of Culture, and museums devoted to Moldavian literature and ancient history. The Church of the Three Hierarchs contains gold mosaics, enameled icons, and candelabras. Arablike stone carvings grace the outside walls.

The city has been an intellectual center since the days of Prince Vasile Lupu, who was known as an outstanding sponsor of the arts in the seventeenth century. That tradition remains today.

CONSTANŢA

Constanţa, Dobrogea's most important port on the Black Sea, is also one of Romania's oldest cities. When founded in the sixth century B.C. by Greek traders, the port was used for exporting slaves and farm products and importing consumer goods from Greece and Rome. The Greeks called the city Tomis. It came under Roman rule in 72 B.C. The Roman Emperor Constantine renamed the city in memory of his favorite sister, Constantina.

The Roman poet Ovid was exiled here in 9 B.C. He spent his last years there writing some of his best works, but also complaining about his difficult life. Today his statue stands in the middle of a city square that bears his name.

In the fourteenth century, Constanţa was merely a pile of stones

Scenes of the port at Constanţa on the Black Sea, Romania's largest seaport, (above and below left) and a statue to the Roman poet Ovid, who spent the last years of his life here (below right)

Central Constanţa

and rubble left by successive barbarian invasions. Disgraced
public officials were sent there as punishment.

By the late nineteenth century, the city began to grow again and
reestablish itself as a seaport for exporting the region's produce.
Aristocrats built summer homes there and shipping trade
increased. The laying of a pipeline from the oil fields of Ploieşti to
Constanţa marked the beginning of the city's industrialization.
Today it thrives as a port of entry for many foreign ships. These
port activities have had a profound effect on Romania's ability to
develop and maintain contacts with world powers outside the
Communist Bloc countries. In the 1960s—as part of its policy to
free itself from Soviet control—Romania began expanding its
trade with Western European nations and the United States.

Some of the antiquities discovered in Constanţa

Today, however, Romania's chief trading partners are still the former Soviet republics.

As excavations for buildings progress, Roman, Greek, Turkish, and other antiquities are discovered. For instance, a very large section of mosaic floor that was part of a Roman market has been unearthed and incorporated in the Dobrogea Regional Museum. Many other vestiges of the past remain as well. Services are still held in an old mosque. A Greek Orthodox church and a synagogue are also in use. A nineteenth-century casino became a Palace of Culture, housing not only gaming tables, but theaters and restaurants as well.

THE BLACK SEA RESORTS

In contrast to industrialized Constanța are the resort cities on the Black Sea. A few miles north of Constanța stands Mamaia, with five miles (eight kilometers) of beaches and an ideal climate. Built on a sandbar between the Black Sea and Lake Siutghiol, it was developed after World War II. Its many hotels and motels of gleaming glass, chrome, and concrete, and its restaurants, shopping centers, nightclubs, and discos bear a remarkable likeness to Miami Beach in Florida.

There are several legends about how Mamaia got its name. The most romantic and repeated tale is of a Turkish caliph who fell in love with a beautiful, but already married, princess. He decided to kidnap her and take her away by sea. As he whisked the princess away, he accidentally awakened her daughter, who ran after her mother crying, "Mamaia, Mamaia." It is not known whether the princess was ever rescued, but this is a favorite story nonetheless.

South of Constanța are the resorts of Eforie Nord, Eforie Sud, Neptun, and, almost at the Bulgarian border, Mangalia. They are popular because they are located near lakes thought to have health-giving qualities in their mud.

CLASSICAL SITES

Inland from the coast are countless relics from the area's past. At Adamclisi is the giant of antiquities, Trajan's Monument. It was built by that Roman emperor to commemorate his victory over the Dacians in A.D. 106. Details and personalities of the campaign are recorded on forty-nine limestone metopes that

An aerial view of the resort city of Mamaia (left) and a Roman statue discovered at Adamclisi

decorate the circular monument, which is 102 feet (31 meters) in diameter and 131 feet (40 meters) high.

At the oldest classical site, Histria, many ruins attest to the antiquity of the area: Greek and Roman wall fragments, marble roads rutted by chariot wheels, a temple of Aphrodite, a temple of Zeus with Ionic columns, a Roman forum, mosaics, sculptures, and an aqueduct built in the second century. The city disappeared around A.D. 630 to 640, until the site was discovered by Romanian archaeologist Vesile Pirran in 1914. By 1948, most of it had been uncovered.

Mangalia boasts a cliff-top promenade lined with Romanian-style hotels constructed mostly since 1958. Still visible are the remains of the Turkish quarter, built when the city was known as Kallatis. The Esmanah Sultan Mosque, erected in 1460, was in memory of the Sultan's daughter.

Above: Steel and iron works in Hunedoara Below: A textile factory in Bucharest

Chapter 5

MAKING THE MOST OF IT

World War II changed the lives of many Romanians. Since 1945, this previously agricultural nation had been industrialized to such an extent that industry accounted for approximately 60 percent of the gross national product. Oil refineries, automobile factories, chemical plants, modern apartment and office buildings, and shopping centers sprang up throughout the nation. Since the government made farms collective, many young farmers moved to cities to take factory jobs while patterns of life significantly changed for those who remained in the rural areas. Romanian agriculture, once prosperous, became plagued by general economic mismanagement.

RESOURCES

Romania has a wide variety of natural resources. Among the most abundant are oil, natural gas, and timber. There are many valuable minerals, too, such as bauxite, coal, copper, lead, silver, and zinc. The country is able to earn hard currency by selling these assets to other countries. Romanians use this currency to buy the products necessary to run their industries. Since World War II, emphasis had been on power, mining, forestry operations, construction materials, and chemical processing. However, in order to capitalize on all these industries, Romania had been forced to import such things as iron ore and coke, mostly from the then Soviet Union. Foreign trade with non-Communist countries had been increasing, but so was Romania's debt to the Western world, from whom they had borrowed vast amounts of money.

AGRICULTURE

Since the end of World War II, planning officials and party theorists had been struggling with the problem of where to put their priorities and how to develop their resources. The major stumbling blocks had been a huge bureaucracy and shortage of hard currency. The decision to emphasize industrialization brought hardships—especially to the farmer. Farm products were being exported because they, too, were a source of hard currency, thus creating food shortages for the consumer at home.

Romania was long regarded as the breadbasket of Eastern Europe, because of its very long growing season and abundant harvests. Constant summer heat, which averages 75 to 85 degrees Fahrenheit (23.9 to 29.4 degrees Celsius), and adequate rainfall are excellent for growing corn and wheat, the two most important crops. Potatoes and sugar beets are also important crops.

Sixty-three percent of the land area of Romania was used for agriculture, which employed about 30 percent of the people at that time.

Collective farming came to Romania with the advent of communism. Until then, farms had always been in the hands of

Harvesting on a collective farm

landowners, who employed peasant workers. But then private landholdings were confiscated and made into giant collective farms owned by the government. They were modeled after the Russian *kolkhozes* (collectives). The government leased the land, directed its use, and sold its products at prices the government controlled. Farmers on the collectives were paid a portion of the earnings. Eighty percent of Romania's farms were then collective.

Another type of socialized farming was the state farm which was run on industrial-management principles, and used as model or experimental farms. A small percentage of farms, mostly high in the mountains where accessibility was difficult, were privately owned.

Collective farming did not resolve Romania's problems. Government management was inefficient and farmers had to rely on old fashioned equipment. The government provided more modern equipment to state owned farms.

After the 1989 revolution, the new government passed land-reform

A state farm near Bucharest

laws that allowed some collective farms to be broken up and given back to previous owners. Land-reform laws did not break up state farms. Eventually, a majority of farms are to be privately owned.

TOURISM

Tourism was one of the most lucrative means of earning much-needed hard currency. Romanians put great effort into dispelling Westerners' preconceived uncomplimentary notions of Communist countries. Tourists were encouraged to travel the country and were reasonably unrestricted as to destinations. There are some 48,000 miles (77,249 kilometers) of roads, although only about 20 percent are modernized. Trains are Romania's chief means of long-distance travel. Being government owned, they often proved to be time-consuming and frustrating due to seemingly unnecessary rules and regulations. Buses still provide most transportation within cities, as fewer than 2 percent of Romanians own a car. Taron, the national airline, is located in Bucharest.

A passenger train (left) and a family car (right) that is given tender loving care

In later years under Ceausescu, tourism in Romania lost its superficial polish and sophistication. Western travelers to the country complained about the rude treatment they encountered on the part of officials. Romanians are a friendly and warm people, but became cautious about engaging in conversations with tourists. Happily that has changed. In 1990 citizens themselves were given rights to travel freely and over 3 million passports were issued.

DOING BUSINESS

Formalities and procedures for doing business in Communist Romania often frustrated Western-oriented businessmen. Channels of bureaucracy were involved and often defied reason. In recent years the government made concerted efforts to lure more foreign enterprise to Romania. In June 1990 a 10-year treaty of economic cooperation was signed with the EEC, and in July the USA's trade agreement was extended for 3 years. Foreign investors can freely establish joint ventures or privately owned domestic companies.

Romanians, clockwise from above, include a young family,
an older man, a group of gypsies, and a grandmother and grandchild

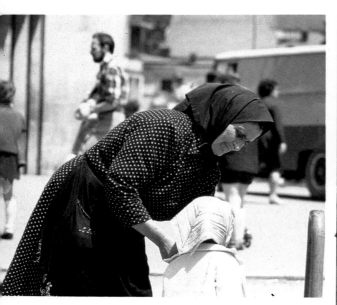

Chapter 6
EVERYDAY LIFE

LANGUAGES AND NATIONALITIES

More than twenty-three million people live in Romania in an area a little smaller than the state of Oregon or the once Federal Republic of Germany. Most proudly claim the ancient Dacians or Emperor Trajan's Roman legions as their ancestors. The Romanian language is a Romance language. It retains the flavor of Latin, sprinkled with traces of French, Italian, Portuguese, and Spanish. It resembles many Western European tongues, which are also derived from Latin. Long ago, the language was written in Cyrillic script. Some examples are still found in the Russian Church (built in 1906) and some of the older buildings in Bucharest.

Romania's population includes about 1.6 million Hungarians, most of whom live in Transylvania. Other nationalities include Germans, Serbo-Croats, and Ukrainians. Except in Transylvania, where Hungarian and Romanian are the predominant languages, most Romanians speak French as a second language. Some also speak German.

The University of Bucharest

EDUCATION

Illiteracy is almost nonexistent. Ninety-eight percent of the population can read and write. Education is free and compulsory for ten years. All children, regardless of social background, attend school. Many teachers spend two to three years in the countryside in small towns to insure that all children do receive education. Students who show interest and aptitude in specialized fields are encouraged to continue their education at no expense to them or their families. Others choose to study vocational courses. These students learn the basic skills that are needed for work on farms or in factories.

Translations of world literature into Romanian are readily available and widely read. Shortages of paper intermittently curtail publishing, and higher prices of books and magazines have been recently adopted.

A lilac festival (left) and folk dancers (above)

Romania has more than one hundred facilities for higher education. This includes seven universities and five technical institutes.

HOLIDAYS

Holidays in Romania usually mean a two-day celebration. The official ones are Labor Day, May 1 and 2, and Romanian Independence Day, August 23 and 24. The New Year holiday is January 1 and 2.

Christmas in the countryside is celebrated in the traditional way. Christmas carols of ancient origin, called *colinda*, are sung. The children of the villages parade through the streets carrying a large paper star, a symbol of the Star of Bethlehem. Even though most Romanian families do not have many luxuries, Christmas is a special time for family feasting and celebration.

The New Year celebration includes a custom known as *plugusorul*. Boys dressed in colorful sheepskin outfits pull a small plow, a *plugusor*, through the villages, wishing everyone good health and good fortune for the coming year.

At traditional festivals throughout the year, Romanians dance to the lively sounds of folk music that was influenced by the melodies of nomadic Gypsies who once roamed the country. The colorful folk culture of the people adds to the country's charm.

YOUTH GROUPS

Under Communist party ideology, most children aged from nine to fourteen usually belonged to an organization called Young Pioneers. The group was easily identifiable by their bright red ties. They were trained in the spirit of Romanian Communism.

Another organization operated by the Communist party was the Union of Communist Youth. The party dispensed political ideas and party directives to the young adults aged from fourteen to twenty-six who belonged to this group.

Both of these groups were designed to occupy children after normal school hours and to act as a training ground for future party members. Youth group members were often required to spend time each week in workshops or on collective farms that also operated as paramilitary bodies. With the dissolution of the party in 1990, these organizations no longer exist.

Romania now maintains a relatively large army of approximately 180,000 troops, basically regarded as defensive forces. At times the army may be called upon for civilian construction work. A smaller navy and air force are also maintained. Some amount of time is compulsory in the armed services. In April 1991 Romania and Russia signed a treaty of friendship and cooperation, each pledging to respect the other's borders.

Dr. Ana Aslam and a member of her staff

HEALTH CARE

Romanians on the whole are health conscious. Many spas and
health resorts throughout the country are popular with
vacationers year round. In Bucharest is the widely acclaimed
Geriatric Institute, headed by Dr. Ana Aslam. Until 1988 she
claimed to have discovered a mysterious "elixir of youth," a
rejuvenating drug. Romanians and foreigners alike attended the
institute.

On the other hand, an elderly peasant may take a less scientific
view and reveal his secret of longevity as "yogurt every day to
live to one hundred years."

Medical care in Romania is beset with problems. Under the
Ceausescu regime, health standards severely declined and medical
services were neglected. Western medicines could not be obtained
and Romanian prescriptions were very expensive. Medical
researchers were denied the possibility to travel abroad, and
contacts with Western physicians were scarce. There were not

enough doctors or hospital beds and, as in many other countries, the majority were located only in the larger cities. However, clinic facilities are being established in the countryside now. Reports have come from Western visitors that some hospitals were rat-infested, filthy, and foul-smelling. Recently the EU has offered some $7 million to assist in the pediatric AIDS epidemic and provide care for at least 100,000 orphans found living in squalid orphanages once run by the state. Health is improving.

RELIGION

Religion is important to the Romanian people, but was strongly controlled by the Ceausescu government. However, in order to avoid popular protests, the prerevolution Communists allowed churches to operate as long as the churches avoided political activities. Religious institutions were manipulated to identify with the party's values. Even though many important churches and some monasteries were destroyed in both Bucharest and in small villages, the church was permitted to train priests and nuns. Because the church identifies with certain cultural traditions, the government considered it an asset to promoting nationalism. However, following the revolution, churches have been granted complete religious freedom.

Eighty percent of the Romanian people belong to the Romanian Orthodox church. The Greek Orthodox church, to which about 10 percent of the people belonged, was incorporated into the Romanian Orthodox church in 1948 by government decree. The rest of the population are Calvinists, Jews, Baptists, and Lutherans.

A good portion of Romanian folk art is embroidered or painted on wood.

FOLK ART AND CUSTOMS

Folk art has taken many forms in Romania and varies from region to region. But bright colors and geometric designs dominate most artistic work. Handmade rugs, intricately decorated Easter eggs, pottery, and wooden sculptures reveal the peasants' artistic talents. Men's sheepskin vests, worn over white shirts, are also heavily embroidered. Gaily colored folk costumes feature elegantly hand-embroidered blouses worked with gold and silver threads and trimmed with spangles and miniature beads of tinted glass.

Even the simplest cottage is decorated with intricate carving on the outside. Gateposts and the ends of rafters and beams show off the owner's craftsmanship. Any home may be a museum of handmade articles. The wealth of a peasant often is measured by the quality and variety of these decorations. A bride's dowry is made up of handmade linens and embroidery.

A gypsy musician playing a dulcimer (left) and a group dancing the hora *(above)*

Handwoven Oltanian rugs are known the world over for their rich designs. The center of each rug usually shows geometric designs and is framed by wide borders with familiar birds, animals, or flowers.

Many traditional customs persist in spite of the modernization and Westernization of Romania. Goods and livestock are sold at market fairs. There are country festivals with music and dancing, and a Girls' Fair each July presents marriageable girls from remote villages to potential suitors.

Romania's national dance is the *hora,* a chain dance done in a circle. From various regions come lively men's dances and those done in pairs and groups. Each region also has its own collection of songs called *doine,* which are usually sad.

In Transylvania each spring, peasants still observe the sheep-counting festival, *Simbra Oilor,* when the sheep are readied for summer grazing higher in the mountains. It is celebrated by all-day feasting and the consumption of a great quantity of *tuica,* the potent Romanian plum brandy.

Traditionally, Romanian married women wear their hair covered by a naframa.

Village weddings follow traditions that have been handed down through the generations, although they may differ slightly from village to village. They are always on Sunday, and the entire village is summoned to the festivities by horsemen who ride around to announce when the wedding will take place. Besides the bride and groom, participants in the wedding include parents, grandparents, godparents, the matchmaker, the best men, who attend and assist the groom with his wedding attire, maids of honor (*drustes*), who do the same for the bride, speakers (*colacari*), cooks (*coltelnica*), cup-bearers, who keep the wine and tuica flowing, standard bearers, who direct the parading, horsemen and their mounts with handwoven saddle blankets, fiddlers, and a variety of other musicians.

Hair styles are of great importance to Romanian women. Various styles denote different regions, but generally maidens wear their hair plaited, and wives wear their hair covered by a *naframa*, a kerchief of silk or cotton.

Wedding preparations begin early in the morning and continue until noon, when the ceremonies begin. The braiding of the bride's hair is meticulously done according to an age-old technique. She wears a coronet decorated with flowers, leaves, semiprecious stones, and multicolored ribbons.

The bridegroom, too, is dressed for the occasion in a vest of white kidskin embroidered and decorated with strands of colored leather. His hat is covered with feathers, flowers, and fir tree branches. His beard is shaved off by his best man to show that he has left the ranks of his bachelor friends and has joined the men. The best man also is ready with the standard to be carried in the procession. It is a tall pole hung with handkerchiefs and bells.

There is a ritual, called the forgiveness ceremony, in which the young couple asks their parents and relatives to forgive them for leaving the family fold. A bard recites a poem:

Take leave, young bride,
From your father, from your mother,
From your brothers, from your sisters,
From the flower garden, too.

Following the church ceremony, lavish feasting and celebrating begin. Wine is served from elegantly carved and painted wooden kegs known as *plosti* and tuica flows from earthen jugs.

The band that plays during the feasting is composed of specific instruments and plays continuously. It includes pan pipes (*nai*), dulcimer (*tembal*), a small double bass (*gorduna*), and violins.

A specially baked loaf of bread as big as a cartwheel is shared by the bride and groom, who also share the same spoon and plate. As they eat the bread, they are showered with grains of corn and the

Above: A wedding party approaching the church   Below: Both the bride and groom wear special clothing for the ceremony.

Rural Romanians milking sheep and doing their laundry in a stream

bread is sprinkled with water, symbols of a life of plenty.

Sometime during the wedding day, the bride is "kidnapped" and the groom is obliged to pay ransom in money, wine, or goods, to retrieve her.

Around midnight there is a bride's dance called *gaina*. During the dance, a hen is brought in adorned with flowers and green leaves, a sign of fertility. It is also a signal to give the wedding gifts to the newlyweds.

The bride and groom are then permitted to leave, but are awakened at dawn by the fiddlers and singers. The bride appears with her hair now tied in a kerchief to show that she has entered womanhood. Feasting begins again and lasts till noon, when the wedding celebration comes to an end.

RURAL AND URBAN LIFE

In other ways as well, rural Romania has remained virtually unchanged for centuries. Peasants still find themselves underpaid

Left: A peasant woman spinning raw wool into yarn
Right: Gypsy women in their colorful clothing

and overworked. Many still live in two- or three-room wooden cottages without plumbing or electricity.

But the folk art decorating the cottages adds a little zest, as do social occasions such as weddings, christenings, and holidays. Peasants wear their most colorful and elaborately embroidered folk costumes to these events.

It's not unusual to pass through villages and find women at the roadside spinning wool just as it has been done for centuries past. They'll gladly show you how it's done. You may come across a gypsy caravan, too, camped just off the road, getting the fire started for the noon meal. Gypsy women, in their long skirts of bright green, purple, and red, and men, in white shirts with bright sashes, seem like a ray of sunshine against the bland coloring of the landscape. Curiosity brings out an entire village should a car stop for information in the more remote sections of the country. The peasants are naturally friendly, but directions, though readily offered, are mostly hearsay from the few who have had an opportunity to go to the larger cities.

High-rise apartments and modern dress in Bucharest

The contrast between rural and urban Romania is dramatic. Western culture has invaded the larger cities. Many people wear Western-style clothes and dance to Western-style music. There are bowling alleys, miniature golf courses, swimming pools, and recreation centers.

High-rise apartments and office buildings line wide avenues. Under Ceausescu, the obsession with saving energy turned Romanian cities into dark citadels. During the winter months it was almost impossible to get a cab and people complained about the freezing temperatures in their barely heated apartments where thermostats could not be turned higher because fuel was in short supply. Use of electricity was also strictly controlled and only low-wattage light bulbs allowed.

For the suburbanite whose wages were low by Western standards, apartment rents were also low. However, apartments

A vendor of lottery tickets

were, and still are, scarce. In efforts to retire foreign debt, Ceausescu rationed basic products the populace needed for living. Although in short supply, agricultural products were exported. This made shopping and waiting in long lines for every purchase a daily task, as items were seldom available. Energy was rationed while fuel was exported. There were only two hours of daily TV programs. A big attraction was the state-run lottery with hopes of winning.

Following the 1989 overthrow of Ceausescu, the new government sought to correct severe economic problems by instituting a free market system rather than state-owned companies. These policies eventually caused much higher prices for consumer goods, soaring inflation, lower wages, unemployment and crippling strikes.

CHILDREN AND CHILD-CARE

According to Ceausescu, "child-bearing is a patriotic duty." One of Ceausescu's main objectives was to increase the birthrate so that the population of Romania would reach thirty million by the

Schoolchildren

year 2000, from its then twenty-two million. In line with this goal, abortion was outlawed and the sale of birth-control products banned. Those who disobeyed could face a prison term.

Ceausescu set a minimum number of five children for each family and instituted strict laws and tax penalties for those who did not conform. Monthly medical examinations were required of women up to the age of forty-five, presumably to insure that they had not had abortions. If they refused, they were denied medical and dental care, which were state controlled.

To insure that people cooperated, door-to-door census takers periodically checked on every family's intimate life-style. If a family refused to answer questions, they might later be visited by the police who would warn of possible criminal charges.

Because Romania is a society in which everyone works, nursery schools and day-care centers, called *crèches*, were an important part of the system. Parents left children for the day or the workweek in the care of trained women at state-provided facilities. These centers were hopelessly inadequate for the

A day-care center

large numbers of children they had to serve. Bribes were often exchanged for better care.

One of the most comprehensive centers was located at the Scinteia complex in Bucharest, where offspring of the privileged benefitted from special attention, although all activities were basically regimented.

Following the coup to overthrow Ceausescu, Romania was left with nearly 100,000 orphans living in squalid conditions. A ban on foreign adoptions was lifted in order to provide homes for them. However, when free-market economic problems developed, many poor Romanian families began to sell their children for living money. An adoption committee was then formed to control adoptions.

A folk dance is performed for the patrons of an outdoor restaurant in Bucharest.

WHAT'S TO EAT?

Both old Romanian traditions and modern, Western culture are part of city life. Many people enjoy going to restaurants, concert halls where Romanian folk music is played, and exhibits of rural Romanian art. Many city dwellers, especially the young, like rock music and Western movies, plays and books. Michael Jackson's 1992 concert complete with flamboyant special effects was a major event.

Before the revolt of 1989 when the Communist government was in charge of nearly every business, restaurant fare became very limited as austerity measures were enforced. The following list of traditional Romanian dishes was unaffordable for many, or just unavailable. As the economy recovers, these traditions will surely flourish again.

Mamaliga, a cornmeal mush that brings back memories of steaming bowls of farina, was the staple of the Romanian diet and

Left: Some of the foods served at Eastertime
Right: Buying sweets on the street in Bucharest

was served in as many ways as the imagination can dream up—
with butter, cheese, sour cream, sugar, or poached eggs—and with
every meal.

Most meals start out with *mititei*, a grilled, garlic-seasoned
sausage, or with *ciorba*, a tangy soup that could be a meal in itself.
This basic soup is combined with sour cream, sauerkraut juice, or
sour fruit juice. The ingredients can be chicken, meatballs, giblets,
meat and potatoes, meat and lots of vegetables, or fish, depending
on the region of the country.

Cabbage is one of the most abundant vegetables, and a popular
dish is *sarmale*, meatballs wrapped in cabbage leaves. *Ghiveci*, a
potpourri of vegetables cooked in oil and served hot or cold,
makes a substantial side dish.

Dessert is a real treat. Although ice cream is popular, the
Romanian speciality is *clatite*, a dessert-type pancake served with
jam or cheese. Coffee is Turkish style, thick and sweet—a
holdover from the Turkish occupation.

Fresh produce for sale in the market

Meals are accompanied by excellent Romanian wine from the Murfatlar vineyards near the Black Sea, tuica, the potent national brandy, beer, or Pepsi-Cola, which came to Romania in 1967, presumably as an attraction for tourists. It was actually an astute move on the part of the Romanians to show Russia that Romania's economic ties with the West were growing stronger.

Homecooked meals revolve around most of the same dishes—thick soups, stews, stuffed cabbage, baked vegetable casseroles, and mamaliga. The Romanians prefer large breakfasts and lunches and usually a light supper of leftovers. These meals often include excellent homemade tuica.

FUN AND GAMES

As in Latin countries, Romania's favorite pastime is the *corso*, or promenade. On warm summer nights, it's hard to believe anyone stays home. The continuing housing shortage has caused several families to share apartments, and there is not much room for privacy. Hence, many take to the outdoors.

Cultural and sporting events are inexpensive, frequent, and very popular. Under the Communist party, physical education, sports

A ski resort in the mountains

and educational committees built sports facilities and urged people to take advantage of them. Individual and team sports continue to be popular with participants and spectators alike. Soccer, tennis, rugby and volleyball lead the list, along with the traditional Romanian sport called *oina*, a game resembling baseball.

In Bucharest there is a large sports arena along with an outdoor theater and ice skating rink. Many people take advantage of the excellent facilities for hiking, camping, and skiing in the magnificent mountain areas.

Outstanding Romanian athletes like tennis star Ilie Nastase and Olympics gymnast Nadia Comaneci, have won distinction throughout the world. At the 1992 Summer Olympics held in Barcelona, Spain, Romanians won medals in various events, including: women's fencing, gymnastics, men's rowing, shooting, and weightlifting.

Above: The fifteenth-century frescoes on the exterior of the Bucovinian monastery in Voronet. Below: A detail from the frescoes

Chapter 7

THE CULTURAL SCENE

ARTS AND CULTURE

The earliest forms of literature were songs that were not written but sung, passed from generation to generation. They ranged from love songs to praise of feats of bravery. Before the nineteenth century, all art was religious in character. Art was developed and carried on behind the security of the monasteries' walls and maintained by the Orthodox church. The oldest written documents were in Slavic, but as the Reformation started to spread to Moldavia and Wallachia, they began to appear in Romanian.

Moldavia's painted monasteries are among the best examples of church-inspired art. Icons provide further examples of early religious works. Peasants paint them today just as they did hundreds of years ago. They depict saints and other religious figures alongside peasants plowing fields or doing everyday chores.

During the nineteenth century, nonreligious art began to appear. Many artists went to France, but they invariably turned to the folk traditions of their native land for inspiration, and their achievements became known beyond the borders of Romania. Artists used Romanian subjects characteristic of their times — gypsies, shepherds, peasants, and village fairs.

During the period between the two world wars, Romanian art knew an unprecedented blossoming. Romanian writers and painters were directly linked to the most active circles of the European avant-garde.

Through the centuries, there were many attempts to stifle Romanian creativity. Creative activity was repressed by various foreign invasions. The arrival of the Russians and communism in 1945 brought the policy known as "Socialist Realism," the theory that all art should make a positive contribution to the progress of the Socialist state. Abstract painting was forbidden. Factories, workbenches, and collective farms became the only subjects acceptable to the state. Every work of art, literature, and music was closely examined by the party to make sure it contained nothing negative about the Soviets or communism. This discouraging situation prompted many talented Romanians to flee to the West to gain more artistic freedom. Since the 1960s, the government has allowed artists more freedom, and art began to flourish again in Romania. Since the revolt of 1989, there is no government censorship. Old Romanian themes and styles appear again, along with much more modern styles. Much current work deals with themes such as humanity's relation to the universe.

Romanian talents, both numerous and impressive, gained recognition in the West. Despite the constant repression they had experienced in Romania, there are some who made names for

A film studio

themselves in various fields. The twentieth century has produced several artists, writers, and musicians known the world over.

CONSTANTIN BRANCUSI

Sculptor Constantin Brancusi, a pioneer of abstract art, was born in a village near Tîrgu-Jiu in 1876. His childhood as a shepherd made him aware of the beauty and moods of nature. This appreciation stayed with him throughout his lifetime and is reflected in his works. He became a carpenter's apprentice and then entered the Bucharest Academy of Fine Arts. At the age of twenty-six, he went on foot to Paris and enrolled in the École des Beaux-Arts.

Two of Brancusi's stone works, The Kissing Gate *and the* Table of Silence, *are part of a group of his sculptures placed in the open in Tîrgu-Jiu.*

The French sculptor Auguste Rodin immediately recognized his talent, but Brancusi turned down an invitation to join Rodin's studio. Instead, he earned his living as a dishwasher and worked at his art on his own. He worked in stone, marble, steel, and wood, and his elemental forms always express something from the folklore of his native Romania.

Eventually, Brancusi gained a worldwide reputation as one of the greatest sculptors of the century. He was invited back to his homeland to create some sculptures for the park in Tîrgu-Jiu. He made *The Kissing Gate* and the *Table of Silence* for the park and, in the center of town, the *Endless Column.*

Brancusi died in 1957 in Paris. His works are now on display in cities around the United States and France.

George Enescu and the museum dedicated to him in Bucharest

GEORGE ENESCU

Romanian composers owe a large debt to their native folk music. The best-known composer is George Enescu, who was also a conductor, violinist, and pianist. His music recalls the haunting traditional melodies of the Romanian countryside and Gypsy violins. His *Romanian Rhapsodies* have gained worldwide recognition.

Enescu was born in 1881. He gave his first public recital when he was thirteen years old. From then on, his rise to fame was rapid. He studied in Paris and Vienna and made many tours in Europe and the United States, appearing often with the New York Philharmonic Orchestra. When he died in 1955, his furniture, piano, and compositions were put on display in a museum in Bucharest that is devoted entirely to his life and accomplishments. The Athenaeum concert hall is the home of the George Enescu Philharmonic Orchestra.

Eugene Ionesco

EUGENE IONESCO

The theater has become an exciting form of entertainment today. The avant-garde plays of modern dramatist Eugene Ionesco are extremely popular. Ionesco went to France when he was young and still lives there. His fantasy world ideas helped give rise to a movement known as the Theater of the Absurd. *Rhinoceros* and *The Bald Soprano* are two of his best-known works.

OTHERS

There are others. The classic Romanian plays of Ion Luca Caragiale are enthusiastically received. Nicolae Grigorescu, who died in 1907, is generally considered the greatest of all Romanian painters. His seascapes of Brittany were done during a stay in France, but he returned to Romania to concentrate on life there. He painted mainly country scenes in the traditional bright colors characteristic of peasant art. Another influential Romanian painter was Ion Andreescu.

Between the two World Wars, patriotic messages began to appear that went along nicely with the Communist philosophy after World War II. The poet Tudor Arghezi altered his melancholy writing style to poems of optimism about peasant revolts. Tristan Tzara, who fled to France to escape conscription, was active in the Dada movement. He wrote in French about the Romanian countryside where he was born.

The writings of both Ion Creanga and Mihail Sadoveanu have been published in the West and are gaining recognition outside their own country. The works of Romania's national poet, Mihai Eminescu, who died in 1889, have been translated into many languages. His poetry draws on folklore and Romanian history to proclaim his ideas of moral and national unity. There is a bust of Eminescu on the shores of the Black Sea at Constanța. It is gazing out at the sea that inspired much of his writings.

LOOKING AHEAD

Today Romania is a country in transition. Despite retirement of much of the foreign debt under Ceausescu's dictatorship, it was at tremendous cost to the economy and people. While living in wealth and enforcing austerity measures, Ceausescu had taken no steps to improve industries within the country. As a result, the

A village in the Carpathian mountains

An onion-domed wayside shrine at the entrance to a village

new government discovered that it had inherited an economy of severe problems. Efforts continue in attempts to establish free-market enterprise. It will be necessary for the government to subsidize basic foods, energy, rent and essential services for at least the coming year. Gradually wages and pensions will be indexed to inflation and privatization of business will lead to foreign investment. The government has requested, but not yet received, most-favored-nation trade status. Despite progress, hard times still cause dissatisfaction with government. In 1992 King Michael, who had been exiled in 1947, was allowed to return to celebrate Easter in Romania. Thousands enthusiastically greeted the royal family, many calling for restoration of the monarchy.

Throughout history life has been difficult for Romanians. One hopes they will continue to call on their rich cultural traditions and determination, to flourish and conquer overwhelming problems.

Name	Ref
Adjud	B8
Aiud	B6
Alba Iulia	B6
Alexandria	D7
Anina	C5
Arad	B5
Argeșul River	C7, C8
Arieșul River	B6
Babadag	C9
Bacău	B8
Baia-Mare	B6
Băilești	C6
Balș	C7
Barladul River	B8
Beiuș	B6
Bihor (mountain peak)	B6
Bîrlad	B8
Bistrița	B7
Bistrița River	B7
Black Sea	C9, D9
Blaj	B6
Botoșani	B8
Bozovici	C5
Brad	B6
Brăila	C8
Brașov	C7
Bucharest (București)	C8
Buhuși	B8
Buzău River	C8
Calafat	D6
Călărași	C8
Caracal	C7
Caransebeș	C6
Carei	B6
Cernavodă	C9
Chișineu-Criș	B5
Cîmpina	C7
Cîmpulung	C7
Cîmpulung Moldovenesc	B7
Cluj-Napoca	B6
Constanța	C9
Corabia	D7
Craiova	C6
Crasna River	B6
Crisul Alb River	B5, B6
Curtea-de-Argeș	C7
Curtici	B5
Danube River	C8
Darabani	A8
Dej	B6
Deva	C6
Dîmbovița River	C7
Dorohoi	B8
Drăgănești	C7
Drăgășani	C7
Eforie	C9
Făgăras	C7
Fălciu	B8
Fălticeni	B8
Fetești	C8
Focșani	C8
Găești	C7
Galați	C9
Gheorgheni	B7
Gherla	B6
Giurgiu	D7
Gura-Humorului	B7
Hațeg	C6
Hîrlău	B8
Hîrșova	C8
Huedin	B6
Hunedoara	C6
Huși	B9
Ialomița River	C7, C8
Iași	B8
Iron Gate	C6
Isaccea	C9
Jijja River	B8
Jiu River	C6
Lipova	B5
Lugoj	C5
Lupeni	C6
Macin	C9
Mangalia	D9
Mărășești	C8
Medgidia	C9
Mediaș	B7
Mihai-Viteazu	C9
Mizil	C8
Moinești	B8
Moldova River	B8
Moldoveanu (mountain peak)	C7
Motrul River	C6
Mureșul River	B5, C6, B7
Nădlac	B5
Negru Vodă	D9
Ocna Sibiului	C7
Ocnele Mari	C7
Odobesti	C8
Odorhei	B7
Oltenița	C8
Oltetul River	C6
Oltul River	C7, D7
Oradea	B5
Orăștie	C6
Oravița	C5
Orșova	C6
Ostrov	C8
Pașcani	B8
Petroșeni	C6
Piatra-Neamț	B8
Pitești	C7
Plenița	C6
Ploiești	C8
Prut River	C8, B9
Rădăuți	B7
Reghin	B7
Reșița	C5
Rîmnicu-Sărat	C8
Rîmnicu-Vîlcea	C7
Roman	B8
Rosiorii-de-Vede	C7
Rosul Pass	C6
Salonta	B5
Satu-Mare	B6
Săven	B8
Sebeș	C6
Sfîntul-Gheorghe	C7
Sibiu	C7
Sighet	B6
Sighișoara	B7
Simleul-Silvanie	B6
Sinaia	C7
Sînnicolau-Mare	B5
Siret	B8
Siretul River	B8
Slănic	C7
Slatina	C7
Slobozia	C8
Someșul River	B6, B7
Stefănești	B8
Strehaia	C6
Suceava	B8
Sulina	C9
Tăndărei	C8
Techirghiol	C9
Tecuci	C8
Teleorman River	C7
Timișoara	C5
Tîrgoviște	C7
Tîrgu-Frumos	B8
Tîrgu-Jiu	C6
Tîrgu-Mureș	B7
Tîrgu-Neamț	B8
Tîrgu-Ocna	B8
Tîrgu-Secuesc	B8
Tîrnava Mica River	B6, B7
Tîrnăveni	B7
Tulcea	C9
Turda	B6
Turnu-Măgurele	D7
Turnu-Severin	C6
Urziceni	C8
Vasile Roaită	C9
Vaslui	B8
Vatra-Dornei	B7
Vedea River	C7
Viziru	C8
Zalău	B6
Zimnicea	D7

MINI-FACTS AT A GLANCE

GENERAL INFORMATION

Official Name: Republic of Romania

Capital: Bucharest

Official Language: Romanian

Government: Until December 1989, Romania's government had been led in all functions by the Romanian Communist party which was established in 1921. The country was a socialist republic built on the Constitution of 1965. In December 1989, the government was overthrown, the president executed and the Congress of the Romanian Communist party was dissolved.

On November 21, 1991, a new Constitution was adopted. A December 8, 1991, nationwide referendum overwhelmingly endorsed the new document. Among the constitution's provisions are guarantees for free speech, pluralism, human rights, privacy and the protection of private property. The death penalty for crimes is banned.

The new constitution calls for a separation of powers among an executive branch headed by the president, a legislative branch and a judiciary. Presidents are limited to two four-year terms and not allowed to belong to a political party while in office. The president, who is popularly elected, appoints a prime minister who must have the support of the majority of the legislature. The prime minister heads a twenty-three-member cabinet. The legislature consists of two houses, a Senate and Chamber of Deputies. A Supreme Court heads the judicial branch of government. The Supreme Court of Justice is the "defender of the people." Justices are nominated to six-year terms by the president with the nominees subject to the approval of Parliament.

Religion: Most Romanians are members of the Greek Orthodox church. The principal religious minorities are the Roman Catholics. Calvinists, Lutherans, Unitarians, and Jews. Following the overthrow of the communist government with state control in 1989, churches have been granted complete religious freedom.

Flag: The 1992 Romanian flag has three vertical stripes of blue, yellow, and red, which are the national colors, and a new coat of arms.

National Anthem: "Trei Culori" ("Three Colours"). A new anthem is now under consideration.

Money: The basic unit is the leu. In March 1994, one leu equaled approximately six U.S. cents.

Weights and Measures: Romania uses the metric system.

Population: Estimated 1994 population: 23,703,000; 47 percent rural, 53 percent urban. 1992 census population: 22,760,449

Cities:

Bucharest 2,350,000
Constanța 350,476
Iași 342,994
Timișoara 334,278
Cluj-Napoca 328,008
Galați 325,788
Brașov 323,825
(Population figures based on 1992 census)

GEOGRAPHY

Highest Point: Mount Moldoveanu, 8,343 ft. (2,543 m) above sea level

Lowest Point: Sea level

Rivers: Transylvania and the Bihor Mountains are drained westward toward the Hungarian plain, where the Someșul, Mureșul, and other rivers empty into the Tisza and the Danube. Some short rivers in Wallachia drain into the Danube as well. Moldavia is drained by the Siretul and the Prut.

Mountains: The Carpathian mountain system dominates the Romanian landscape. It extends from Ukraine in the north to Yugoslavia in the southwest. The Transylvanian Alps run east to west.

Climate: The climate is continental with hot summers and cold winters. Most of the annual rainfall occurs during the summer. Bucharest has an average temperature of 26° F. (-3° C) in January and 73° F. (23° C) in July. Temperatures are more moderate in the mountains. The plains of Moldavia and Dobrogea are dry and are exposed to bitter winter winds that blow from the Russian steppe.

Greatest Distances: East to west—about 450 mi. (724 k)
North to south—about 320 mi. (515 k)
Coastline—130 mi. (209 k)

Area: 91,700 sq. mi. (237,500 km²)

NATURE

Trees: Forests cover about a quarter of the country. Oaks predominate at about 2,600 ft. (791 m), beeches between 2,600 and 4,600 ft. (791 and 1,402 m), and conifers between 4,600 and 5,900 ft. (1,402 and 1,798 m). At the highest levels there are alpine and subalpine pastures.

Animals: Animal life is rich and varied. Some rare types are found in the alpine heights of the Carpathians. Forest animals include brown bear, red deer, wolf, fox, lynx, wild pig, marten, and various songbirds. Eagles, vultures, and falcons are found in more isolated areas.

The lower course of the Danube is rich in animal, bird, and fish life. Carp are plentiful and sturgeon, rich in caviar, flourish.

EVERYDAY LIFE

Food: Grilled meats, including sausages (*mititei*) are popular. *Ciorba* is a filling, tangy soup. Corn-meal mush (*mamaliga*) or bread is cooked and served in many different ways. Cabbage is plentiful and the basis of many dishes; *sarmale*, meatballs wrapped in cabbage leaves, is one of the most popular. A favorite dessert is *clatite*, a pancake served with jam or cheese. Wine and a plain brandy called *tuica* are also popular. Lately, food shortages have become a main feature of Romanian life.

Housing: There is a housing shortage in the cities. Many city buildings are hundreds of years old, but there are also many modern structures built since industrialization began. Most rural Romanians live in two- or three-room wooden cottages, plain and simple, but decorated with attractive wall rugs, wood-carved furniture, and colorfully decorated plates.

Holidays:

New Year's, January 1-2
Labor Day, May 1-2

Culture: Modern Romanian culture has a personality of its own. Because of the country's location, cultural influences contributed to its spiritual diversity. The early Roman influence, which made Romania part of the Latin world, was soon challenged by Slav, Turkish, Greek, and Hungarian influences. Byzantine influence was profound also during the Middle Ages, and it can be seen in church ritual, architecture, iconography, and fresco painting. During the sixteenth and seventeenth centuries, a great deal of ecclesiastical literature was written in Romanian.

Literature and art flourished during the last part of the nineteenth century. The poet Mihai Eminescu, storyteller Ion Creanga, dramatist Ion Luca Caragiale, and critic Titu Maiorescu are the most widely respected. The most prominent artists were Theodor Aman, a portraitist, landscapists Nicolae Grigorescu and Ion Andreescu, and Stefan Luchian, a painter of suburban life.

Though Western literacy and artistic movements did have an impact on Romania between World Wars I and II, Romanian culture remained native, and its interwar writers never became known abroad. Tristan Tzara, however, who fled to France to avoid conscription, was active in the Dada movement. The interwar writers easily adapted themselves to the philosophy and aims of the Communist regime. Tudor

Arghezi, a poet of the human condition, and Mihail Sadoveanu, a writer of historical novels, continued to publish under the Communist regime. The playwright Eugene Ionesco, whose most famous plays are *The Bald Soprano* and *Rhinoceros*, is known throughout the world.

The Communist regime, since 1965, became less critical of unorthodox forms of literary expression, even those imitative of Western authors, provided they were not offensive to communism. However, after 1971, a new wave of Stalinism was launched and Romanian writers were summoned to celebrate socialism. Postwar literature also has seen an increase in the number of works published in Hungarian. Sculptor Constantin Brancusi, who lived and created in France, is represented in most of the major museums of the world.

In music, an effort was made to encourage "seizing the various aspects of Socialist life." In recent years, however, the Romanian government encouraged the revival of the works of George Enescu and other classical composers. Experiments in modern music were developed in recent years.

The theater is Romania's most lively art form. Outstanding performances of classic Romanian works, such as those of Ion Luca Caragiale, as well as plays by modern or avant-garde Romanian and international playwrights, find sophisticated audiences in the many theaters of the capital and of the smaller cities. Since the revolt of 1989 there has been no government control over the arts.

Wood carvings, brightly ornamented costumes, carpets, and pottery, and other elements of Romanian folk culture remain popular and have become known throughout the world. Folk art is characterized by abstract or geometric designs and stylized representations of plants and animals.

Sports and Recreation: Sporting events are inexpensive, popular, and frequent. Soccer is the most popular spectator sport in Romania. Romanians have two favorite vacation spots—the mountains and the Black Sea Coast. Skiing, hiking, mountain climbing, and gorgeous scenery are the major attractions of the mountains, while swimming and relaxing in the sun are the attractions of the sea.

Communication: Local telephone service is automatic and fairly dependable. International connections are fairly good, though there are often delays and the costs are outrageously expensive. There are about 490 newspapers and magazines published throughout the country, as well as about 40 papers of regional and ethnic interest. There are also about four million television sets and two million telephones. The quality of TV programs is poor and Romanians usually watch the broadcasts of the neighboring Bulgarian television.

Transportation: Railways provide the main method of transportation for both freight and passengers. Since World War II, diesel and electric motors have been placed in service, and the major lines have been electrified. Roads largely have been brought up to modern standards.

Romania has maritime connections with many countries, and the port of Constanţa plays a major role in the national economy. The Danube River is a major transportation route.

Bucharest is the main center for air transportation. The majority of flights by the national airline, Tarom, are to Europe, North Africa, and the Middle East. Since 1990, a percentage of privatization is in process with businesses.

Schools: Education is free and universal, and compulsory for ten years, and its development has been the key to the economic transformation of the country and to the gradual elimination of illiteracy. After the required general school, children can attend middle schools (general or specialized, four or five years) or one of a wide range of technical or professional schools or institutes of higher education. The educational system is no longer controlled by the Communist party.

The University of Bucharest was found in 1864. Other important schools are Babes-Bolyai University in Cluj-Napoca and the Polytechnic Institute in Bucharest.

The major institution of academic research is the Academy of the Republic of Romania. Its publishing house, Editura Academiei, produces research papers and journals. The academy's library contains more than 7,000,000 volumes.

Health and Welfare: Romanians are very health conscious, and there are many spas and health resorts around the country. But health care is very poor. There is a scarcity of drugs and Romanians must pay high prices for better medical treatment. Most major medical facilities are concentrated in larger cities with many smaller villages having no facilities. This situation is improving as construction of new hospitals increases. The quality of medical care has improved with the training of more doctors, but health services are still poor. The standard of living is still low and many kinds of sophisticated medical treatment are not available.

Principal Products:

Agriculture: Corn, potatoes, wheat, fruits
Industry: Clothing, food, machinery, iron ore, natural gas, petroleum and petroleum products

IMPORTANT DATES

300s B.C.—Dacians live in what is now Romania

A.D. 100s—Romania becomes a province of the Roman Empire

275—Rome officially withdraws from the Romanian territory

200s to 1100s—Romania invaded by Barbarians

1250 to 1350—Moldavia and Wallachia gradually become independent principalities

c. 1500—The principalities ruled by Turks

1601—First unification of Wallachia, Moldavia, and Transylvania under Prince Michael the Brave

1829—Turkish rule ends as Russian troops occupy Romania

1834—Russian troops withdraw from the principalities

1859—Prince Alexander Cuza elected as common ruler of Moldavia and Wallachia

1861—Moldavia and Wallachia officially unite and form the nation of Romania

1866—Cuza forced to resign and replaced by Karl of Hohenzollern, who takes the name Prince Carol

1878—Romania's full independence from Turkey is recognized

1881—Romania becomes a kingdom, and Carol becomes King Carol I

1907—Romania's peasants revolt

1914—Romania almost doubles in size as it is joined by Transylvania and other surrounding lands as a result of the Paris Peace Treaty

1927—King Ferdinand dies

1940—After the Soviet occupation of Bessarabia, Romania joins the German side in World War II; King Carol gives up his throne and his son Michael becomes king

1944—The tide of the war turns; Romania joins the Allied side

1947—King Michael gives up his throne; Romania becomes a Communist country ruled by the Romanian Workers' party headed by Gheorghe Gheorghiu-Dej

1961—Romania initiates cultural and educational exchanges with the United States.

1965—Gheorghe Gheorghiu-Dej's successor, Nicolae Ceausescu, presents a new constitution

1969—Richard Nixon travels to Romania—the first American president to visit a Communist country since 1945

1970—Romania signs a friendship treaty with Russia, while continuing to seek good relations with the West

1972—Romania joins the World Bank

1975—Romania gains most-favored-nation status in trade agreements with the United States.

1977—An earthquake strikes the Bucharest area causing about 1,500 deaths and extensive property damage

1989—Communist government begins bulldozing 5,000 small villages in order to create 500 large agricultural city-trade centers; Romanians revolt and the Communist party is dissolved; Nicolae Ceausescu and his wife are executed and most of their family and party members are imprisoned

1990—Ion Iliescu becomes president of the Republic of Romania

1991—A new constitution guaranteeing human rights is overwhelmingly endorsed; Prime Minister Petre Roman resigns from office and Theodor Stologan is appointed

1992—The foreign ministers of Romania and Germany sign treaties of friendship and cooperation; King Michael, in exile since 1947, is allowed to return to Romania to celebrate Easter; Ion Iliescu is reelected president; After Theodor Stologan steps down, Ion Iliescu appoints Nicolae Vacaroiu as prime minister

1994—Nearly 2 million workers (one-fifth of the work force) join the two largest unions in general strikes to protest lack of progress in econimic reforms; the IMF approves $700 million in loans after Romania promises to reduce inflation and privatize more businesses; a communications satellite TV network is launched to operate from Bucharest, broadcasting news and entertainment for 12 hours each day; in a general vote, Moldova rejects union with Romania

IMPORTANT PEOPLE

Theodor Aman (1831-91), portraitist

Ion Andreescu (1850-82), landscape painter

Tudor Arghezi (1880-1967), great Romanian poet

Ana Aslan (1897-1988), doctor, head of the Geriatric Institute in Bucharest

General Ion Antonescu (1882-1946)

Constantin Brancoveanu (1654-1714), medieval prince of Wallachia

Constantin Brancusi (1876-1957), world-famous sculptor

Ion Luca Caragiale (1852-1912), writer and author of satirical comedies

King Carol I (1839-1914), (Karl of Hohenzollern), first king of Romania (1881-1914)

King Carol II (1893-1953), king (1930-40)

Nicolae Ceausescu (1918-1989) head of Romania between 1967-89

Nadia Comaneci, world-renowned Olympic gymnast

Ion Creanga (1837-89), storyteller

Prince Alexander Cuza (1820-73), first ruler of Romania

Mihai Eminescu (1850-89), poet, considered to be foremost Romanian man of letters

George Enescu (1881-1955), violinist, composer, and conductor; teacher of violinist Yehudi Menuhin

Ferdinand I (1865-1927), king of Romania (1914-27)

Gheorghe Gheorghiu-Dej (1901-65), general secretary of the Communist party (1944-65)

Nicolae Grigorescu (1838-1907), landscape painter

Eugene Ionesco (1909-1994), playwright of international distinction

Stefan Luchian (1868-1916), painter of suburban life

Titu Maiorescu (1840-1917), critic

King Michael, (1921-   ), king (1929-30, 1940-47); abdicated in 1947

Michael the Brave, Wallachian ruler between 1593-1601

Mircea the Old, Wallachian prince (1386-1418)

Ilie Nastase, tennis star

Vasile Parvan (1882-1927), archaeologist who in 1914 discovered the site of the classical city of Histria

Mihail Sadoveanu (1880-1970s), historical novelist

Stephan the Great, Prince of Moldavia from 1457-1504

Bram Stoker (1847-1912), Irish writer who published *Nosferatu*

Vlad Tepes (Vlad the Impaler) (d. 1476), ruler of Wallachia (1456-62, 1476-77); considered the basis for the legend of Dracula

Tristan Tzara (1896-1963), Romanian-born essayist, poet, and editor; leader in the Dada movement

Women in Bucharest

A farmhouse near Moldavia

INDEX

Page numbers that appear in boldface type indicate illustrations

About the Author

Betty Carran, a native of Cleveland, Ohio is a freelance photo journalist who has traveled extensively in many of the lesser-known regions of the world. She started her professional photographic career as a portrait photographer while still in high school. Before her marriage, she attended Northwestern University and Cleveland Institute of Art.

Her love of travel has taken her not only to the well-known Western European countries, but to places as diverse as Africa, the Orient, South America, and Russia, including Siberia. She has recorded her travels in writing as well as on film, which has enabled her to provide insight into many different cultures. Her two sons have accompanied her on several trips.

Betty owns and manages her own real estate development business in Cleveland. When she is not actively involved in the day-to-day business operations, she manages to do volunteer work for several Cleveland-area charitable organizations. She is a lifelong patron of the arts and in her leisure time enjoys doing needlepoint, and playing tennis and golf.